Oregon Bible Records
from
Museums
of the
Willamette Valley

Volume 1

Jo Ann Burgess

HERITAGE BOOKS
2024

HERITAGE BOOKS
AN IMPRINT OF HERITAGE BOOKS, INC.

Books, CDs, and more—Worldwide

For our listing of thousands of titles see our website
at
www.HeritageBooks.com

Published 2024 by
HERITAGE BOOKS, INC.
Publishing Division
5810 Ruatan Street
Berwyn Heights, MD 20740

Copyright © 1988 Jo Ann Burgess

All rights reserved. No part of this book may be reproduced or transmitted in any form or by any means, electronic or mechanical, including photocopying, recording or by any information storage and retrieval system without written permission from the author, except for the inclusion of brief quotations in a review.

International Standard Book Number
Paperbound: 978-1-55613-134-9

ACKNOWLEDGEMENTS

The museums of the Willamette Valley are testimonies to the pride which the Oregonians have for the history of their state. Dedicated individuals have spent countless hours preserving and organizing the manuscripts and artifacts of the area. These same people are eager to share their knowledge of the history of their communities with others. Not only was I welcomed by the staff of all the museums but all extended extra effort to locate the information I needed to complete this compilation. I am grateful for this help but especially I admire the workers' dedication.

I especially want to thank Judy Rycraft Juntunen, Manuscripts Librarian of the Benton County Historical Museum, for the help she provided. Her knowledge of and willingness to share the documents in the Benton County collection greatly enriched this compilation or records.

ABBREVIATIONS

1-H	One handwriting
1-WI	One writing implement
VH	Varied Handwriting
VWI	Varied Writing Implements

Ja	January	My	May	S	September
F	February	Je	June	Oc	October
Mr	March	Jl	July	N	November
Ap	April	Ag	August	D	December

b.	Birth	m.	Married	d.	Died

Zip Code abbreviations indicate states
En England   Fr France   Gy Germany

****

MYERS FAMILY RECORD

****

Surnames
  Hathaway   Rybolt
  Myers
Places
  Avoca, IA   McLean Co., IL
  Des Moines, IA   Pottawattamie Co.,
  McLean, IL   IA

THE HOLY BIBLE. Chicago: Louis Lloyd & Co., ca. 1873. 1-H, VWI: Cottage Grove Historical Museum. Cottage Grove, Oregon.

Inscription:
  Presented to Miss Emma L. Hathaway by mem-bers of "Union Congregational Church, of McLean, McLean County, Illinois, Oct. 4th 1875. As a memento, or memorial of her faithful services as organist in said Church. John C. Rybolt, Pastor.

Births:
  Aida Emma, 25 Ja 1882 Avoca, Pottawattamie
    County, Iowa
  Nellie Alice, 29 Ja 1886, Avoca

Myers Marriage Certificate:
  This is to certify that George Myers of Des Moines in the State of Iowa and Emma L. Hathaway of McLean in the State of Illinois were by me united together in Holy Matrimony on the Sixth day of October in the year of our Lord One Thousand Eight Hundred and Seventy five. In presence of: Mrs. Mary Rybolt, Miss M. S. Rybolt. John C. Rybolt, Officiating Minister.

****

BODINE FAMILY RECORD

****

Surnames
  Bodine
  Burkhart
  Foster
  Fry
  Haley
  Hite
  Hoel
  Hunter
  Lochridge
  Markham
  Richardson
  Rickert
  Safley
  Umphrey
Places
  Albany, OR
  Corvallis, OR
  Indiana
  Linn Co., OR
  Pennsylvania

THE HOLY BIBLE. New York: American Bible Society, 1883. VH, VWI: Cottage Grove Historical Museum. Cottage Grove, Oregon.

Inscription:
  William A. Bodine "Mizpak" Gen, 81-49 Your Sister, May 26th 1---
Marriages:
  William Albert Bodine and Sarah Adiline Richardson, 27 Ja 1886, at residence of Albert Umphrey, Linn Co., OR
  Ruth Lenora Bodine and Burkhart
  Margarette Isabelle Bodine and Frank Safley
  Nettie Naomie Bodine and Hoel
  Addie Elizabeth Bodine and Laurence Rickert, 11 N 1920
  Veinetta Bodine and Chester Hite, 4 May '30
Births:
  William Albert Bodine, 18 Jl 1858, Albany, OR
  Sarah Adiline Richardson, 6 Mr 1865

Daniel Harvie Bodine, 23 Oc 1886
Ruth Lenora Bodine, 22 Oc 1889
Margarette Isabelle Bodine, 4 Je 1891

Nettie Naomi Bodine, 25 Ap 1897
Addie Elizabeth Bodine, 13 S 1899
Veinetta Bodine, 30 Oc 1906
Deaths:
  William Albert Bodine, 1919, Albany, New York [1919, Albany, New York in different hand]
  Sarah Adiline Richardson, 26 Je 1943, Corvallis, OR

Ruth Lenora Bodine, 7 D 1858
Nettie Naomi Bodine, 17 Oc 66
Notes:
Contained within the Bible were loose notebook pages with the following information:

Marriages:
  William A. Bodine and Matilda Hunter, 14 S 1820
Births:
  William A. Bodine, 8 Mr 1794
  Matilda Bodine, 13 Ag 1805
  Elizabeth Ann Bodine, 13 Mr 1822
  Charles Buchanan Bodine, 11 Mr 1825
  Daniel Har(vy) Bodine, 24 S 1827, IN
  Sarah Jane Bodine, 17 Ja 1830
  Julia Dorcas Bodine, 1 D 1831
  Hanah Scovel Bodine, 19 Oc 1833
  William Alworth Bodine, 4 Oc 1835
  Alvira E. Bodine, 14 Jl 1838
  Francis Bodine, 27 N 1840
  Samuel S. Bodine, 29 Oc 1842
  David Stewart Bodine, 9 Je 1845
  Matilda Susan Bodine, 11 My 1847
Deaths:
  Samuel S. Bodine, 25 N 1863, 21y 26d
  Elizabeth Ann Lochridge, 6 Mr 1863, 46y 9m 23d
  Daniel Harvy Bodine, 9 Sept. 1869, 41y 11m 15d, Albany
  Matilda Bodine, 26 N 1877 in the 73 year

of her age
William A. Bodine, 17 Oc 1883
David Stewart Bodine, 17 Ag 1871

Notes:
Daniel Harvy Bodine was born in Ind. 1822, died in Albany 1869. Arrived in Albany 1854-worked as a carpner for a few years in Albany. Bought a farm of Haley. 4m east of Albany, 160 acres, where he died 1869. Young Foster was born in Penn., 1827. Arrived in Albany fall 1850. Margaretta Bodine, Mary Fry, and I, Libby Markham 3 sisters - Brothers was William, Robert, John, James. There first winter in Albany only 13 people in town. 5 women and 8 men, 4 men being Fosters, two others ...

****

POWELL FAMILY RECORD

****

Surnames
  Alkine
  Alkire
  Bracken
  Churchill
  Davis
  Geer
  Goble
  Harris
  Hendee
  Hughes
  Ingle
  Lane
  Lowe
  Maxwell
  McKnight
  McReynolds
  Nation
  Overholser
  Powell
  Propst
  Ramsey
  Schwar
  Searbery
  Shime
  Small
  Smallwood
  Southerland
  Taylor
  Wright

Places
  Illinois
  Ohio
  Virginia

[No title page remained in the Bible] VH, VWI: Cottage Grove Historical Museum. Cottage Grove, Oregon.

Alexander H. Powell and Mary A. McKnight, 23 F 1864
Belle Powell and Henry Taylor, 4 Je 1887
Alfred S. Powell and Emma Taylor, 4 S 1887
Florence Winona Powell and Alexander Small, 28 Ag 1895
Matilda Powell and Lincoln Taylor, 22 Jl 1896
Lester Winfred and Pearl Wright, 21 Jl 1910
Lester Winfred A. Powell and Myrtle M. Searbery, 12 D 1931

Rev. John Alkine and Susan Nation, 1780
Joseph Powell and Sarah Alkire, 4 Oc 1804
Alfred Powell and Sarah Bracken, 1834

Births:
A. H. Powell, 8 D 1834
M. A. Powell, 4 Ap 1844
Sarah M. Powell, 6 My 1865
Alfred S. Powell, 6 Mr 1867
Clarinda B. Powell, 12 D 1869
Florence W. Powell, 14 Jl 1876
Lester A. W. Powell, 29 N 1881

John Alkine, 1759

Grandchildren:
Ray A. Taylor, 12 Mr 1888, d/of Belle
Roma E. Powell, 5 S 1888, d/of Alfred
Winona Ruth Taylor, 20 Mr 1892, d/of Belle
Norman Elsworth Taylor, 14 Jl 1894, s/of Belle
Robin Taylor Powell, 3 Oc 1892, s/of Alfred
Anabel Small, 20 D 1896, d/of Florence
Mary Lois Small, 17 N 1901, d/of Florence
Marjorie Florence Small, 13 Oc 1903, d/of Florence
Dorothea Belle Taylor, 5 Ap 1897, d/of Belle

Carroll Powell Taylor, 16 D 1900, s/of Belle
Lawrence Henry Taylor, 6 My 1906, s/of Belle
Virgil Alexander Powell, 12 Ja 1900, s/of Alfred
Erwin Alexander Small, 9 Oc 1908, d/of Florence
Wendell Powell Small, 17 S 1918

Deaths:
Roma Ethel Powell, 4 F 1889
Mary Ann Powell (McKnight), 31 My 1912
Alexander Hamilton Powell, 13 Mr 1915
Erwin Alexander Small, 19 Ja 1929
George [blank] Small, 13 Ja 1923
Florence Winona Small, 26 Ja 1945
Lester Winfred A. Powell, 17 Je 1958

John Alkine, 1836
Susan Nation, 1832

Memoranda:
Record of Joseph Powell of Virginia.
Joseph Powell was born 13 F 1784
Sarah Alkire was born 24 D 1786
Joseph and Sarah, his wife, were married 4 Oc 1804

Births:
Thirza Powell, 28 Je 1805, Ingle
John A. Powell, 20 F 1807
Noah Powell, 24 S 1808
Alfred Powell, 10 Jl 1810
Cyntha Powell Ingle, 10 Mr 1812
Suzanna Powell Hughes, 23 Oc 1813
Ivy Powell, 3 N 1815, Smallwood 1815
Lucinda Powell Propst, 19 F 1817
Abel Powell, 28 N 1818
Samuel, 13 F 1820
Dolly Powell, 26 Oc 1821
Sally Powell Schwar, 4 Je 1823
Elizabeth Powell, 17 D 1825
Deborah Powell Lowe, 25 S 1827
Joseph Powell, 6 N 1830

Deaths:
Alfred Powell, 18 D 1881
Sarah Powell Bracken, 1837

Note:
  Alfred Powell was born in Ohio came to Illinois in 1824 [4 crossed out 5 written beside] to Oregon 1851.

Record of Alfred Powell of Ohio to Ill 1825:
  Marriages:
    Alfred Powell and Sarah Bracken, 1834
    Alfred Powell and Hanna Shime (Goble), 1838
    Alfred Powell and Abigail Lane, 1860
    Alfred Powell and Mary Churchill, Oc 1874
    James Powell and Martha Harris, Ja 1866
    Alexander Powell and Mary McKnight, 25 F 1864
    Joseph Powell and Malissa Ramsey, 25 S 1862
    Ruth Powell and Qwen Maxwell, 1856
    Nancy Powell and Antony Maxwell, 1860
    Polly Powell and Henry Ramsey, Ja 62
    Jane Powell and Burton Davis, Ap 1869
  Births:
    Alfred Powell, 10 Jl 1810
    Sarah Powell (Bracken), 30 N 1815
    Alexander H., 8 D 1834
    James H., 9 Ja 1837
    Ruth Powell (Maxwell), 30 Je 1839 [1834 crossed out]
    Joseph Goble Powell, 1 Je 1841
    Nancy Powell (Maxwell) 6 My 1843
    Polly Powell (Ramsey), 1 Ja 1846
    Jane Powell (Davis), 16 D 1849
  Deaths:
    Alfred Powell, 18 D 1881
    Sarah Powell (Bracken), Jan 1837
    James H., 29 D 1880
    Nancy Powell (Maxwell), 24 Ap 1902
    Polly Powell (Ramsey), 14 Jl 1900
    Abigail Powell (Lane), 13 D 1873
    Ruth Powell, F 1868
Record of Joseph Powell
  Marriages:
    Joseph Powell and Malissa Ramsey, 1846

Emma Powell and Stephen Overholser, 14 F 1889
Nancy Powell and John Overholser, Ja 1891
Mande (Maude?) Powell and Levi Geer, Je 1891
Ida May and Ernest McReynolds, 1897
George A. and Emma Southerland
Robert B. & Lena Geer
William Edwin and Daisy Hendee, 1910 [also entered Edwin William]
Emily Jane Powell, 1889
Charles Leighton Powell, 26 F 1908
Mande Rose Powell, 21 Je 1896

Births:
Joseph Powell 1 Je 1841
Emily Jane Powell, 3 Ag 1865
Nancy Ann Powell, Ja 1868
Charles Leighton Powell, D 1872
Samuel Powell
Mande Rose Powell, 21 Je 1896
Ida May Powell, 8 My 1877
Claude Powell
George Alfred Powell
Robert Burnett Powell
Edwin William Powell, 15 F 1889
James Henry Powell, 17 S 1891
   Children of Levi and Mande Geer
     Joseph Levi
     Robert Samuel
     Cecil Ray
Violetta Melissa Overholser, 23 Ja 1890
Leroy Leighton Overholser, 24 Oc 1891
Gladys Sarah Overholser, 1 Je 1898
Wayne Porris Overholser, 4 S 1906

Deaths:
Mande Rose Powell, 3 Jl 1907

****

McKNIGHT FAMILY RECORD

****

Surnames
- Bautalo
- Frank
- McKnight
- Newe
- Powell
- Skidmore
- Taylor
- Wilson

THE HOLY BIBLE. New York: American Bible Society, 1888. 1-H, 1-WI: Cottage Grove Historical Museum. Cottage Grove, Oregon.

Marriages:
  David McKnight and Matilda Skidmore
    James McKnight
    Parley McKnight
    Sarah McKnight Frank
    John McKnight
    Maryanne McKnight Powell
  James McKnight and Marilla Wilson
  Parley and Julia Newe
  John Alvin McKnight and Martha Bautalo
  Sarah McKnight and John Frank
  Mary McKnight and Alexander Powell, 1864

  Bell Powell and Henry Taylor, 1887
  Alfred Powell and Emma Taylor, 1887
Deaths:
  Jennie Martin McKnight, 1881
  Alvin McKnight
Note:
  Roma Ethel Powell d/of Alfred S., 3 F 1889

****

MOODY FAMILY RECORD

****

Surnames
- Doherty
- James
- McCormack
- McFarlance

Moody   Stephenson
Nicholas   Talene
Places
  Ashland, OR   Morgan Co., IL
  Boone Co., IN   Oregon Territory
  Calapooga, OR   Port Townsend, WA
  Concord, IL   Salem, OR
  Granby, MA   The Dalles, OR
  Jacksonville, IL   Wasco Co., OR
  Josephine Co., OR   Williams, OR
  Linn Co., OR   Woodbine, IA

THE HOLY BIBLE. New York: American Bible Society, 1852. VH, VWI: Cottage Grove Historical Museum. Cottage Grove, Oregon

Marriages:
Page one. Left column
  Zenas F. Moody and Mary J. Stephenson, 19 N 1853, Methodist Epicopal Church, Calapooge, Linn County, Oregon Territory
  Z. A. Moody and Catherine Doherty, 15 My 1892

Page one. Right column
  Wm. H. Moody and Clora McFarlance, 4 Ja 1883, St. Paul's Church, The Dalles, Wasco Co., OR
  R. E. Moody and Beatrice J. James, 12 N 1890, St. Paul's Church, Port Townsend, WA
  Edner Moody and Eugene P. McCormack, 26 Oc 1898, at home of the moth. in Talene
  Adelbert M. Moody and Mabel Nichols, 21 F 1906, Woodbine, IA

Births:
Page one. Left column
  Zenas F. Moody, 27 My 1832, Granby, MA
  Mary Jane Moody, 18 Ap 1836, Boon Co., IN
  Malcohn Adelbert, 30 N 1854, Calapooga, Linn Co., Oregon Territory
  Zenas Arizona, 7 Ap 1857, Concord, Morgan Co., IL
  William Hovey, 5 Oc 1860, Jacksonville, Morgan Co., IL

       Ralp Elmo, 27 Ag 1867, Dalles, Wasco Co.,
       OR
Page one. Right column
   Edna Sid [Sid in different hand and pen],
       8 Jl 1869, Dalles, Wasco Co., OR
   Adelbert Montague, 6 D 1883, The Dalles,
       OR
   Mary Eliza Moody, 10 S 1885, The Dalles,
       OR
   - nedeilla(?) Edna, 25 Oc 1887
Page two. Left Column
   Zenas Ferry, s/of Z. A. and Catharine
       Moody, 26 Mr 1893, at Williams, Josephine Co., OR
   Mary Esther, d/of Z. A. and Catharine
       Moody, 7 Ap 1895, 1 PM
   Edna, d/of Z. A. and Catharine Moody, same
       day, 1:30 PM, near Ashland, OR
   Eugene Doherty, s/of Z. A. and Catharine
       Moody, 18 Ap 1896, 5 AM
   Edith Idalia, d/of Z. A. and Catharine
       Moody, 8 Mr 1899, 5 AM Wed.
Page two. Right Column
   Frances Ferry, ch/of R. E. and B. J.
       Moody, 25 S 1891
Deaths:
Page one. Left Column
   Edna Moody McCormack, 12 Oc 1905, Salem,
       OR, River View Cemetery, Salem, OR
   Mary J. Stephenson, w/of Zenas Ferry
       Moody, 16 Mr 1915, Salem, OR, River View
       Cemetery
   Eugene P. McCormack, 28 Jl 1916, Salem,
       OR, River View Cemetery
   Zenas Ferry Moody, 14 Mr 1917, River Veiw
       Cemetery, Salem, OR
Page two. Right Column
   Mary Eliza Moody, 9 S 1893, Dalles, OR
   Edna Moody (Infant), 7 Ap 1895, Ashland,
       OR
   Mary Esther Moody, 7 My 1895, age 1m Ashland, OR
Museum Card:
   [Bible] belonged to Zenas F. Moody born
   May 27, 1832. Oregon's 7th Governor

****

RYCRAFT FAMILY RECORD

****

Surnames
  Belknap   Nash
  Coyle   Rowland
  Elliott   Rycraft
  Gilbert   Seits
  Hawley   Simpson
  Howard   Starr
  Junkin   Walter
  Knox   Wyatt
  Merrill   Wyrick
  Moss
Places
  Ashland   Lane Co., OR
  Benton Co., OR   Lebanon
  Butler Co., OH   Monroe
  Chaney Valley, NY   New York
  Corvallis   Oregon Territory
  Eugene City, OR   Pennsylvania
  Hillsboro   Perrydale
  Iowa   Portland
  Junction City   Tigard
  Klamath, CA   Van Buren Co., IA

[Copied from photo copy of Bible pages, Case Lockwood, & Co., 1866] VH, VWI: Benton County Historical Museum. Philomath, Oregon.

Marriages:
  S. L. Rycraft and S. J. Hawley, 1 Ag 1858
  Charles A. Rycraft and Pearl R. Seits, 11 Je 1911
  Ruth Rycraft and Erwin Walter, 12 Je 1948

Births:
Page one.
  Squier L. Rycraft, 30 S 1828, Butler Co. OH

Sarah Jane Rycraft, 14 Je 1843, Van Buren Co., IA
Alma May Rycraft, 6 Jl 1859, Benton Co., OR
Emma Francis Rycraft, 5 N 1861, Benton Co., OR
George H. Rycraft, 23 Jl 1863, Benton Co., OR
Jo Chapman Rycraft, 22 Je 1866, Benton Co., OR
John Alphaus Rycraft, 22 D 1867, Benton Co., OR
Leona Bell Rycraft, 25 Mr 1870, Benton Co., OR
Leonidas Hawley Rycraft, 20 Je 1872, Benton Co., OR
Mark Pomeroy Rycraft, 15 Ja 1876, Benton Co., OR

Page two.
Ethel Maud Rycraft, 15 S 1877
Edna Luella Rycraft, 3 Ag 1880
Mildred Beatrice Rycraft, 26 Ap 1883
Charles Arden Rycraft, 15 Ja 1885
Hershel Edwin Rycraft, 4 Je 1919
Ruth Genevieve Rycraft, 30 Mr 19-0
Pearl Seits Rycraft, 7 Jl 1892

Deaths:
Edna Luella Augusta Rycraft, 3 Ap 1882, aged 1y 1m 26d
S. J. Rycraft, 4 Ag 1915
S. L. Rycraft, 4 Mr 1925
Hershel E. Rycraft, 7 F 1935
Frances Rowland, 14 F 1935
George Rycraft, 21 Je 1949

Obituaries:
    Milton A. Wyatt. Lebanon, March 7...died in Lebanon Friday. Interment will be in Mt. Union cemetery, Corvallis.
    Mr. Wyatt was the son of pioneer Oregon residents, Mr. and Mrs. J. E. Wyatt. His mother crossed the plains in a covered wagon in 1853 and his father was a native of the Oregon territory.
    Milton Wyatt was born in Corvallis September 21, 1870. He was graduated

from Oregon Agricultural college in 1895. He operated farms in the Corvallis and Lebanon districts until he retired and moved to Ashland about five years ago.

Survivors include the widow, the former Evalina Merrill, whom he married in 1911 in Portland: three daughters, Mrs. Frances Moss, Ashland; Mrs. Mildred Knox and Mrs. Mabel Wyrick, Lebanon: one son, Norman Wyatt, Klamath, Cal.; three sisters, Mrs. Lizzie Elliott, Perrydale; Mrs. Minnie Junkin Tigard; Mrs. Edna Nash, Corvallis; two brothers, Elbert, Hillsboro, and Ernest, Junction City; and seven grandchildren.

Jane Belknap-wife of Jesse Belknap, died Sunday, Dec. 10, 1876,...She was born in Pennsylvania, 1792; emigrated to Western New York in 1796 with her parents... joined the M. E. Church in her sixteenth year,... She came to Oregon in 1848 with her husband, and settled in Benton County in the neighborhood bearing her name. Herself and husband were the pioneers of Methodism in this western wild. The first annual conference held in Oregon...was that held by Bishop Simpson, and her house was his home. From that time on the house of Jesse Belknap was the preacher's home,... She leaves a large family of children, grand-children, and great-grandchildren. Her husband, now in his 85th year, is still living...

Sewell Hawley. On Monday evening at 7 p. m. near Monroe, Benton county in the Belknap settlement, Sewell R. Hawley died suddenly of rheumatism of the heart. He had been judge of election in the precinct and was just beginning the work of counting the ballots when with a spasmodic gesture of the hands he was instantly, dead;... The deceased was a stalwart man of more than six feet apparently in sound health. He came to Oregon when a boy in the forties with his father, Chatman Hawley, in the Belknap-Gilbert wagon train...He was buried in the neighborhood cemetery being 57 year of age, born February 2, 1839, in Iowa...He leaves a wife, Mrs. Emma A. Hawley, and four children, Mrs. Weltha K. Starr, Mrs. Maria Howard, and Rev. A. L. Hawley, of Monroe, and Prof. W. C. Hawley, of this city. He had long been a member of the Methodist Church... [Ed Note: Penciled in margin, 1896]

Jepe Belknap died at the residence of his son Ransome near Monroe, this county on the 16th day of Nov. A.D. 1881, near 90 years of age. [page torn]...was born in Chaney Valley,...state of New Y---

Mr. W. Coyle, who formerly lived in this county near M------ died recently...at his home about twelve miles east of Portland. Mr. Coyle was an early settler of this county... At the time of his death he must have been about 55 years of age.

Lorenzo Dow Gilbert, who settled on his donation claim about - west of Monroe in this county in the year 1847 died last Sunday...at the residence of his son near Eugene City, Lane Co., Oregon. At the time of his death he was seventy years of age, was the father of a large family of children, most of whom together with his aged wife survive him.

****

RICKARD FAMILY RECORD

****

Surnames
  Clark   Michael
  Fiechter   Rickard
  Johnson   Scruggs
Places
  Benton Co., OR

PEOPLES STANDARD EDITION OF THE HOLY BIBLE. Columbus, Ohio: Wm Garretson & Co., 1876. VH, VWI: Benton County Historical Museum. Philomath, Oregon.

Marriage Certificate:
  This certifies that the rite of holy matrimony was celebrated between Peter Rickard of Benton Co., Oregon and Clarinda Fiechter of Benton Co., Oregon on October 17, 1877 at Arch Johnson's by Rev. E. G. Michael.

Marriages:
  Thella B. Rickard to Amos E. Scruggs, 26 S 1907

Births:
  Peter Rickard, 28 My 1855
  Clarinda Rickard, 15 Ap 1858
  Thella Rickard, 27 Ap 1882
  Mark Rickard, 2 Jl 1884
  Luke Rickard, 5 Oc 1886
  Leatha Rickard, 17 My 1888
  Vena Rickard, 31 Mr 1890
  Julius H. Scruggs, 11 Jl 1914

Deaths:
  Luke Rickard, 28 F 1887
  Vena Rickard Clark, 28 S 1918
  Peter Rickard, 5 My 1936
  Mark Rickard, 6 S 1936
  Clarinda Rickard, 27 Mr 1939

Julius H. Scruggs, Capt., 27 Mr 1946
Thella B. Scuggs, Ja 1976

****

SLATER FAMILY RECORD

****

Surnames
  McCain   Smith
  Slater
Places
  Benton Co., OR   New York City
  Boone Co., KY   Upper Canada
  Dearborn Co., IN   Vermont
  DeKalb Co., IL

[Copied from photo copy of Bible pages, no title page available] VH, VWI: Benton County Historical Museum. Philomath, Oregon.

Births:
Page one.
  Robert Slater, 24 My 1801, Upper Canada
  Laurinda Smith, 17 Mr 1807, Vermont
  Melvina Slater, 28 Jl 1824
  Francis Marion Slater, 26 S 1826
  Ann Eliza Slater, 29 Ag 1828
  Julia Slater, 27 N 1836
  Major Robert Slater, 5 Ja 1833
  Almarinda Slater, 28 My 1835
Page two. Sept. 24th 1848
  Robert Slater, 24 My 1801, Upper Canada
  Laurinda Smith, 17 March 1807, Vermont
                            Second Addited (?)
  Melvina Slater, 28 Jl 1824, Dearborn Co., IN
  Francis Marion Slater, 26 S 1826, Dearborn Co., IN

Ann Eliza Slater, 29 Ag 1828, Dearborn Co., IN
Thankful J. Slater, 27 N 1830, Dearborn Co., IN
Major R. Slater, 5 Ja(?) 1833, Dearborn Co.,IN
Almarinda Slater, 28 May, after hard wind storm, Dearborn, IA [Ed. note: IA was early abbreviation for Indiana]
Laura Slater, 4 F 18--
Hiram Willis Slater, 25 N 1845

Page three. Family record Second
Maranda Jane McCain, 24 S 1841, Boone Co., KY
Clayton McCain, 3 My 1844, DeKalb Co., IL
Lee McCain, 21 F 1819, City of New York

Page four. 1865 Family Record May the 8
Lee McCain, 21 F 1819, City of New York
Melvina Slater, 28 Jl 1824, Dearborn Co., IN
Miranda Jane McCain, 24 S 1841, Boon Co., KY
Clayton McCain, 3 My 1844, DeKalb Co., IL
Selden Ledia McCain, 23 Ag 1854, Benton, OR

Page 5.
Alice Lodoiska McCain, 12 Oc 1856, Benton Co., OR
Amy Florence McCain, 10 Jl 1858, Benton Co., OR
Volney Lucien McCain, 10 Je 1860, Benton Co., OR

Deaths:
Robert Slater, 29 S 1835

****

McCAIN FAMILY RECORD

****

Surnames
- Boyd
- Buckingham
- Dennis
- Dodge
- Fletcher
- Forrest
- Hawley
- McCain
- Mires
- Palmer
- Rycraft
- Simler
- Slater
- Starr
- Vidito
- Williams
- Wood

Places
- Bellfountain, OR
- California
- Illinois
- Indiana
- Kentucky
- Missouri
- New York City
- Ohio
- Oregon
- Pennsylvania

AMY McCAIN FLETCHER JOURNAL
Page one.
Lee McCain was born in the City of New York, 21 F 1819. Died March 22, 1865
Melvina Slater was born in Indiana, 28 Jl 1824. Died 31 Ag 1882
Lee McCain and Melvina Slater was united in marriage
Maranda Jane McCain was born in Kentucky, 24 S 1841. Died 22 S 1866

Clayton McCain was born in Illinois, 3 My 1844
Selden Ledru McCain was born in Oregon, 23 Ag 1854. Died 3 My 1875
Alice Lodoiska McCain was born in Oregon, 12 Oc 1856. Died 25 Je 1890

Page two.
Amy Florence McCain was born in Oregon, 10 Jl 1858. Died 29 Oc 1946
Volney Lucien McCain was born in Oregon, 10 Je 1860. Died 31 Ja 1888

Fanny Dennis was born in -----
Volney L. McCain and Fanny Dennis was united in marriage

Page three.
Amy Florence McCain was born in Oregon, 10 Jl 1858. Died 29 Oc 1946

Eva Lee Fletcher was born in Oregon, 9 F 1880. Died 16 F 1907

Obituary:
Mrs. Marion O. Palmer died at her father's home Saturday, February 16, 1907. She was the wife of Marion O. Palmer and daughter of Mr. and Mrs. W. H. Fletcher. She was a sufferer...[of] tuberculosis. She leaves the husband and little daughter, father and mother and one sister,... The funeral services were held at the home of W. H. Fletcher Monday, February 18, at 1:00 p.m., conducted by Rev. A. M. Williams, pastor of the Presbyterian church of this city. Interment was made in the Masonic cemetery.

Page four.
George Washington Buckingham was born in Ohio, 24 Jl 1840. Died 22 Ap 1900
George W. Buckingham and Alice L. McCain was united in marriage 12 Oc 1874
Florence Pauline Buckingham was born in Oregon, 9 S 1875
Manley Lee Buckingham was born in Oregon, 9 N 1877
Ruby Estella Buckingham was born in Oregon, 12 F 1881. Died 29 Oc 1902

Page five.
Randolph C. Buckingham was born in New(?)---, 4 My 1835. Died 24 My 1863
Mary Ann Boyd was born in Illinois, 28 N 1838
Randolph C. Buckingham and Mary Ann Boyd was united in marriage 19 S 1857
Laura Kinney Buckingham was born in Oregon, 19 Ap 1859
Arthur Boyd Buckingham was born in Oregon, 28 Mr 1861. Died 31 Jl 1886, drowned.

Page six.
  William Henry Palmer was born in Pennsylvania, 16 Oc 1836
  William H. Palmer and Mary A. Boyd Buckingham were united in marriage 14 Jl 1865
  Alice Matilda Palmer was born in Oregon, 24 Mr 1867
  Sarah Lucinda Palmer was born in California, 3 My 1870
  Nancy Elizabeth Palmer was born in Oregon, 23 Ja 1872
  Henry Randolph Palmer was born in Oregon, 6 Ag 1875
  Marion Albert Palmer was born in Oregon, 2 Mr 1878
Page seven.
  Norman Ovando Dodge was born in Oregon, 29 Mr 1862
  Norman O. Dodge and Laura K. Buckingham were united in marriage 29 Mr 1890
  Marion Anna Dodge was born in Oregon, 1 Jl 1891
  Enid Philena Dodge was born in Oregon, 24 S 1895
  Randolph Orvil Dodge was born in Oregon, 29 Mr 1899
Page eight.
  George H. Rycraft was born in Ohio, 22 N 1814. Died 2 Mr 1890
  Maranda Jane McCain and George H. Rycraft was united in marriage 1 Ap 1859
  Kate Alvira Rycraft was born in Oregon, 1 Ja 1860. [Part illegible]--83 left 5 children.
  Harriet Viola Rycraft was born in Oregon, 1 Je 1864. Died 28 Ap 1893. 28y 10m 28d. Married R. G. Mires [Death and marriage information written in different hand]
  Squier Lee Rycraft was born in Oregon, 6 My 1866. Died 6 May 1891. 25 years [Age written in different hand]
Page nine.
  Rachel Vidito was born in Oregon
  Squire Lee Rycraft and Rachel Vidito

were united in marriage
Page ten.
Harry J. Wood was born in California, 30 Ag 1879
Harry J. Wood and Ruby Estella Buckingham were united in marriage 27 F 1901 [Estella inserted in different hand]
Delbert Wright Wood was born in Cal. 6 Mr 1902. Died 12 S 1902
Page eleven.
Sylva Hawley was born in Oregon, 4 Je 1879. Died 11 Ja 1906
Manley Lee Buckingham and Sylva Hawley were united in marriage 27 My 1900
Elda Alice Buckingham was born in Oregon, 4 F 1901. Bellfountain at the home of Geo. W. Buckingham [Place of birth in different hand]
Ruby Ellen Buckingham was born in Oregon, 23 Ag 1902. Bellfountain at the home of Geo W. Buckingham [Place of birth in different hand]
Sylvia Opal Buckingham was born in Ore., 5 F 1904. Bellfountain at the home of Geo. W. Buckingham [Place of birth in different hand]
Page twelve.
George Starr was born in Missouri, 20 Oc 1869 George Starr and Florence Buckingham were united in marriage 20 F 1901
Emmett Earl Starr was born in Oregon, 10 S 1902
Fay McWilliam Starr was born in Orgon, 11 Ag 1904
Inez Starr was born in Oregon, 7 Ag 1906
Orpha was born in Oregon
Amy was born in Oregon, 1910
Page thirteen.
Emma Forrest was born in Oregon, 8 Ag 1880
Isaac C. Simler and Emma Forrest were united in marriage 27 Mr 1889
Icy Luverna Simler was born in Oregon, 9 Ag 1894

McCOY FAMILY RECORD

Surnames
  Haptonstall   Warner
  McCoy   Wyard
  Millrath
Places
  Benton Co., OR   Monroe, OR
  Farmington, WA   Mortensville, OH
  Fayette Co., OH   Oakesdale, WA
  Galle Co., OH   St. Joe, MO
  Indiana   Whitman Co., WA
  Missouri   Willamette Val., OR

[Copied from photo copy of Bible pages, no title page available] VH, VWI: Benton County Historical Society. Philomath, Oregon.

Marriages:
  James McCoy and Margaret Haptonstall, 10 Ap 1851
Births:
  Margaret McCoy, 22 D 1831, Galle Co., OH
Deaths:
  Paulinia McCoy, 12 Oc 1863
  Abrom A. McCoy, 10 N 1863
  Charity C. McCoy, 22 F 1871
  Charity McCoy, 28 S 1862
  Ollie Warner, 25 Jl 1885
  Barlarey Haptonstall, 15 S 1866
  Abraham Haptonstall, 1 S 1853
  Margaret McCoy, 6 N 1913
  William McCoy, 9 My 1931
  Hatty P. Wyard, 13 S 1934
  James Henry McCoy, 14 Oc 1935
  Sam McCoy
  John McCoy, 31 Mr 1959
  Ellen Sherlock Montgomery McCoy

Claude McCoy, s/of Henry & Etna, 29 F 1984, 90 years of age

Obituary:
McCOY-Jas., died Jan. 22, 1897 at his home in Oakesdale, Wash., of paralysis. The funeral services occurred at the M. E. Church,, of which he has been a member since his conversion at the old Bellefontaine campground in Oregon many years ago. Father McCoy was the first Methodist in Oakesdale...He was born in Mortensville, Fayette Co., ...He was born in Mortensville, Fayette Co., Ohio, July 9, 1830, moving from there to Indiana; thence to Missouri in 1840. Crossing the plains in 1853 he located in Benton Co., Oregon where he lived until 1877, when he moved to Whitman Co., Wash, locating upon a farm, upon which now stands the town of Oakesdale. On April 10, 1851 he was married to Miss Margaret Haptenstall,... To them were born nine children, four of whom had passed on before...

Note: Included on marriage page:
Crossed plains from St. Joe, Missouri 1853. Settled in Willamette Valley, Oregon, near Monroe, 1853. Moved to Whitman Co., Wash. 1876, Farmington Wash. Moved to homestead 1877. Oakesdale, Wash. Margaret Lucille McCoy, married July 31st 1938 at home of her father, to Mr. John A. Millrath.

****

HOWELL FAMILY RECORD

****

Surnames
- Cole
- Duchess of Kent
- George III (King)
- Howell
- McConnell
- Miles
- Moses
- Southmayed

Victoria (Queen) Watson
Wallace   Williams
Ward   Wilson
Places
  Arkansas Territory   Pope Co., AR
  England   Van Buren, AR

[Transcribed from a handwritten copy made from a book of Mrs. Anna McConnell. Van Buren, Ark.] 1-H 1WI: Benton County Historical Museum. Philomath, Oregon.

Marriages:
  Laban Clark Howell and Fannie Wilson, 13 F 1817
  Mary Wilson Howell and David Foster Williams, 29 D 1834, Pope Co., Ark.
  Martha Cole Howell and Alfred Wallace, 1 N 1834, Pope Co., AR
  Eleanor L. Howell and Augustus Ward, 27 Ja 1842, Pope Co., AR
  Susannah Richards Howell and Leonard Clay Southmayed, 18 D 1850, Van Buren, AR
  Sarah Ann Howell and William Albert Watson, 19 Oc 1852, at residence of his sister, Martha Watson
  Lucinda Light Howell and Rev. Peter Allan Moses, 5 Ap 1858, Van Buren, AR
  Amasa Brown Howell and Sallie Miles, 24 D 1858

Births:
  Laban Clark Howell, s/of Amasa and Martha Cole Howell, 23 Je 1795
  Fannie (Wilson) Howell, w/of Laban Clark Howell, 24 Oc 1800
  Mary Wilson Howell, 10 Jl 1818, Friday
  Martha Cole Howell, 21 Mr 1820, Tuesday
  Samuel Wilson Howell, 2 Ja 1822, Wednesday
  Elizabeth Howell, 3 Ag 1824
  Eleanor L. Howell, 11 D 1825, Sunday
  Amasa Brown Howell, 7 D 1827, Friday
  Wiley Blount Howell, 5 D 1829, Saturday
  Susanah Richards Howell, 25 Ap 1832, Wednesday
  Sarah Ann Howell, 4 Ap 1834, Friday, Arkansas Territory
  Lucinda Light Howell, 7 Ag 1838, Tuesday

Jesse Leban Howell, 2 Jl 1840, Sunday
Note:
"Grannie" Cole married Stephen Cole in England. Cousin to King George III, Queen Victoria. A daughter of Duchess of Kent. Duchess was youngest daughter of George III.
  Children:
    Martha Cole
    Stephen Cole
Martha married Amasa Howell. She was educated in England before coming to America.
  Children:
    Jesse Howell
    James Howell
    Laban Clark Howell
    Clairborne Howell
    Elizabeth Howell
    Sallie Howell
    Ruth Howell

****

HOWELL FAMILY RECORD

****

Surnames
  Howell
  Miles
  Moses
  Southmayed
  Wallace
  Ward
  Watson
  Williamson
  Wilson
Places
  Alma
  Corvallis, OR
  Fayetteville, AR
  Great Amer. Desert
  Pine Knob, AR
  Prairie Grove, AR
  San Antonio, TX
  Van Buren, AR

[Prepared from a typescript copy made by Mr. D. F. Williamson of Pine Knob, Arkansas, March 4th, 1872, of the records in the family Bible of Laban C. Howell]

Marriages:
  Laban C. Howell and Fanny Wilson, 13 F 1817

  Mary Wilson Howell and D. Foster Williamson, 29 D 1835
  Martha Cole Howell and Alfred Wallace, 7 N 1836
  Eleanor Gaines Howell and Augustus J. Ward, 27 D 1842
  Susan R. Howell and Leonard C. Southmayed, 18 D 1850
  Sarah Ann Howell and William A. Watson, 19 Oc 1852
  Lucinda Light Howell and Peter Moses, 5 Ap 1858
  Amasa Brown Howell and Sarah Miles, 24 D 1858

Births:
  Laban Clark Howell, 23 Je 1795
  Fanny Howell, 24 Oc 1800

  Children of Laban and Fanny Howell
    Mary Wilson Howell, 10 Jl 1818
    Martha Cole Howell, 21 Mr 1820
    Samuel Wilson Howell, 2 Ja 1822
    Elizabeth Howell, 3 Ag 1824
    Eleanor Gaines Howell, 11 D 1825
    Amasa Brown Howell, 7 D 1827
    Willie Blount Howell, 5 D 1829
    Susan Richards Howell, 25 Ap 1832
    Sarah Ann Howell, 4 Ap 1834
    Lucinda Light Howell, 7 Ag 1838
    Jesse Laban Howell, 26 Jl 1840

Deaths:
  Laban Clark Howell, 10 Ap 1845
  Fanny Howell, 30 Ap 1847

  Martha Cole Howell, May 1854, Wednesday
  Samuel Wilson Howell, 23 Oc 1842
  Elizabeth Howell, 14 Ja 1825

Eleanor Gaines Howell, 18 Ag 1889 at Van Buren, Ark
Amasa Brown Howell, 21 S 1881 at Alma, buried Fairview Cemetery, Van Buren, AR
Willie Blount Howell, 8 S 1849, Great American Desert on the road to Oregon
Susan Richards Howell, 1 Oc 1915, Van Buren, Ar
Sarah Ann Howell, 4 Mr 1902, Prairie Grove, Arkansas, buried at Fayetteville
Lucinda Light Howell, 26 Mr 1923, Corvallis, OR, buried Masonic cemetery, Corvallis
Jesse Laban Howell, 7 Ap 1863, San Antonio, Texas

****

MOLYNEUX FAMILY RECORD

****

Surnames
  Bawker
  Bowker
  Emmons
  Hammill
  Molyneaux
  Reamer
  Scott

Places
  Coshocton Co., OH
  Early, IA
  Fountain Co., IN
  Glendale, SD
  Hand Co., SD
  Iroquois Co., IL
  Miller, SD
  Park Co., IN
  Paris, France
  Sac Co., IA
  Sioux City, IA
  Storm Lake, IA
  Vermillion Co., IN

THE HOLY BIBLE. Chicago, IL: Montgomery Ward & Co., 1892 1-H, 1-WI: Benton County Historical Museum. Philomath, Oregon.

Marriages:
  John Molyneux and Amanda F. Emmons, 5 S 1856, Park Co., IN

Robert Scott and Phebe Molyneux, 8 My 1882, Storm Lake, IA
A. C. Bawker and Sarrah J. Molyneux, 1 Ja 1890, Early, IA
Avery Hammill and Marry Molyneux, 8 F 1890, Miller, Hand Co., SD
Aron Reamer and Olie B. Molyneux, My 1892 Sue City [Sioux City]
Murlen A. Hammill and Addie Molyneux, 9 Mr 1902, Glendale, Hand Co., SD

Births:
Left Column
John Molyneux, 18 Mr 1821, Parris, France
Amanda Emmons, 10 Ag 1838, Soction [Coschocton] Co., OH
John F. Molyneux, 29 Oc 1859, Fountain Co., IN
Sarah J. Molyneux, 15 Mr 1861 (Vermilion Co., IN)
Phebe Molyneux, 9 F 1864, Park Co., IN
William Molyneux, 1 Ja 1868, Iroquise Co., IL
Marry M. Molyneux, 8 F 1869, Iroquise Co., IL
Olie B. Molyneux, 19 Oc 1872, Iroquise Co., IL
Adlaide Molyneux, 16 Ag 1875, Livingston Co., IL
Isac E. Molyneux, 20 My 1878, Sac Co., IA
Levie Molyneux, 23 My 1881, Sac Co., IA

Right column
Elvin M. Hammill, 26 D 1902
Maurice Lavel Hammill, 9 Ap 1908
Viola Winifred Hammill, 18 Ja 1910
Elmer Herold Hammill, 23 Je 1911

Deaths:
Elmer Herold Hammill, 28 F 1912
(William Molyneux, 2 Ja 1868, Iroquis Co., IL)
-illey R T Molyneux, 28 Oc 1892 Hand Co., SD
(John Molyneux, 20 S 1898, Miller, SD)

Note:
Bawker alternately spelled Bowker

Loose page in the Bible repeats the information on the family pages except for information shown above in ().

****

HENKLE FAMILY RECORD

****

Surnames
  Armstrong   Henkle
  Barker   King
  Gragg
Places
  Benton Co., OR Ter.   Pendleton Co., VA
  Fayette Co., OH   Shelby Co., OH
  New Virginia

HOLY BIBLE. Philadelphia: McCarty & Davis, 1832. VH, VWI: Benton County Historical Museum. Philomath, Oregon.

Marriages:
  John Henkle and Anna Gragg, 27 D 1808
Births:
  John Henkle, 24 F 1788, Penelton Co. [Pendelton], New Virginia
  Anna Henkle, 18 My 1787, Penelton Co., New Virginia
  Ichabod Henkle, s/of Jacob and Anna, 1 Oc 1810, Pennelton Co., New VA.
  Sidney Henkle, d/of Jacob and Anna, 7 Je 1812, Pennelton Co., New Virginia
  Harriet and Mary, twins, 15 D 1814
  Christenia Henkle, 4 Je 1816, Fayette Co., OH
  William Henkle, 15 My 1819, Fayatt Co., OH
  Mary Henkle, 24 Mr 1822, Fayatt Co., OH
  Jacob Henkle, 1 Oc 1825, OH
  Andrew J. Henkle, 27 My 1828, Shelby Co., OH

Deaths:
- Hariet and Mary, twins of Jacob and Anna Henkle, both died, Mary within 24 hours after birth, and Hariet when three months old, 15 Dec.
- Anna Henkle, w/of Jacob Henkle, 28 Ap 1856, Monday, Benton Co., Oregon Territory, aged 68 years 11 months and 10 days
- Jacob Henkle, 7 Jl 1875, Wednesday, Benton County, Oregon Territoy, aged 87 years 4 months & 13 days
- William Henkle, 21 Jl 1894
- Sidney Henkle Armstrong, 20 D 1847, aged 35 6m 13 day
- Christena Henkle Barker, 22 S 1902, 83 yr 4 mo 7 da
- Ichabod Z. Henkle, 24 Jl 1903, aged 91 9mo 28
- Mary Henkle King, 5 Je 1908, age 86 2mo 12

****

FIECHTER/JOHNSON FAMILY RECORD

****

Surnames
- Baxter
- Brown
- Bryson
- Burr
- Davis
- Fiechter
- Hinkle
- Holder
- Jasper
- Johnson
- Musgrave
- Newton
- Rickard
- Starr
- Thompson

Places
- Corvallis, OR

HOLY BIBLE. New York: American Bible Society, 1869. VH, VWI: Benton County Historical Museum. Philomath, Oregon.

Inscription:
  Cynthia Ellen Johnson. Corvallis, OR, Dec. 25, 1897
Marriages:
  Cynthia Ellen Newton and John Fiechter, 21 Mr 1850 by Rev. John Starr
  Cynthia Ellen Fiechter and Archibald Johnson, 21 Mr 1862 by Mr. Jasper
  Malissa Fiechter and William Hinkle, 7 Oc 1869
  Marion Fiechter and Sarah Brown, Oct
  Emeline Fiechter and William Brown, 7 Oc 1875 by Rev. Baxter
  Clarinda Fiechter and Peter Rickard, Oct.
  Cythia Annie Fiechter and William Burr, June
  Pinkie Daisy Holder and John C. Johnson, 3 Ag 1894 by John Bryson
  Adaline Johnson and Charlie Davis, 12 F 1896 by Dr. Tompson
  Cynthia Anna Johnson and William W. Musgrave, Je 1909
Births:
Left Column
  John Fiechter, 15 Mr 1822
  Cynthia Ellen Newton, 1 Oc 1833
  Malissa Fiechter, 21 Ap 1851 [1 over 2]
  Emeline Fiechter, 12 D 1854
  Marion Fiechter, 14 Jl 1852
  Rachel Fiechter, 4 Jl 1856
  Clarienda Fiechter, 15 Ap 1858
  Cynthia Anne Fiechter, 25 My 1859
  Ellen Ann Fiechter, 25 My 1859
Right Column
  Archibald Johnson, 18 Ja 1833
  Cynthia Ellen Newton, 1 Oc 1833
  Margetta Johnson, 13 F 1863
  John Vinton Johnson, 7 F 1864
  Susan Justina Johnson, 24 My 1866
  Adaline Johnson, 27 D 1869
  Elnora Johnson, 3 Jl 1872
  Archibald Johnson, Jr., 15 Jl 1875
  Cynthia Anna Johnson, 17 Je 1885

Daughters of William W. and Cynthia Anna Musgrave
   Cynthia Ella, Je 1910
   Thelma Ella, D 1911

Deaths:
Left Column
  John Fiechter, 3 Oc 1861
  Rachel Fiechter, 24 Je 1861
  Ellen Ann Fiechter, 1 D 1881

Right Column
  Arichibald Johnson, 22 D 1889
  Margetta Johnson, 9 Oc 1863
  John Vinton Johnson, 31 Ag 1892
  Pinke H. Johnson, 7 Oc 1887

Note:
  Written in margin: 13 children born to Cynthis E. Fiechter-Johnson

  Record on loose page in Bible:
    John Fiechter, 16 Mr 1822
    John Fiechter, died 3 Oct 1861
    Cynthia E. Fiechter, 1 Oct 1833, died 5 F 1924
    Melissa Fiechter, born 21 Ap 1851
    Malisa T. died 11 Ap 1921
    Marion Fiechter born 14 Jl 1852
    Emeline Fiechter born 12 D 1854
    Rachel Fiechter born 4 Jl 1856
    Rachel Fiechter died 24 Je 1861

    Clarienda Fiechter born 15 Ap 1858
    Anna Fiechter born 25 May 1858

    Ann Fiechter also [unfinished line]
    Ann Fiechter died 1 D 1881

****

COX FAMILY RECORD

****

Surnames
   Cox

[Copied from photo copy of Bible pages, no title page available] VH, VWI: Benton County Historical Museum. Philomath, Oregon.

Births:
  John Cox, 1 Oc 1818
  Elijah Cox, 11 Ja 1820
  Jesse Cox, 27 Mr 1821
  Solomon Cox, 1 F 1823
  Harriet Cox, 6 My 1824
  Julatha Cox, 3 F 1826
  Benjamin Cox, 5 Ja 1828
  William N. Cox, 29 Ap 1829
  Mary Cox, 10 D 1830
  Solomon Cox, 29 (?) Mr 1791/2/3 [All three dates appear in the record]
Deaths:
  Margery Cox, 2 Ja 1846, aged 79 years 2 mo, 6 days
  Solomon Cox, 4 Mr 1889, aged 95 years 11 mo 5 days

****

GRAGG FAMILY RECORD

****

Surnames
  Buckingham   Haines
  Gragg   McLain
Places
  Benton Co., OR   Morgan Co., OH
  Des Moines, IA

[Copied from typescript of Bible record, no title page information available]

Marriages:
  Joseph Gragg and Lavina Philena Buckingham, 9 Ja 1863, Benton Co., Or

William Harvey McLain and Betsy Minerva
    Gragg, 28 Ag 1892
  Thomas Heman Gragg and Mary Olive Haines,
    14 S 1892
Births:
  Joseph Gragg, 16 N 1827, Morgan Co., OH
  Lavina P. Gragg, 27 F 1843, Des Moines, IA
  Thomas Heman Gragg, 18 Oc 186-
  Betsy Minerva Gragg, 20 S 1864
  Mary Irene Gragg, 20 Ap 1867
  Cordelia Gertrude Gragg, 7 N 1869
  George Wesley Gragg, 18 Mr 1872
  Joseph Philo Gragg, 13 D 1874
  David Vernon Gragg, 2 Oc 1876
  Marcus Edward Gragg, 28 N 1879
Deaths:
  Mary Irene Gragg, 4 N 1875
  George Wesley Gragg, 13 N 1875
  Cordelia Gertrude Gragg, 14 N 1875

****

MASON FAMILY RECORD

****

Surnames
  Landore   Tycer
  Mason   Weavry
  McCormack

[Title page missing, the New Testament title page reads, Brattleboro, Vt.: Joseph Steen & Co., 1847.] VH, VWI: Linn County Museum. Brownsville, Oregon.

Marriages:
  David Mason and Barbara Weavry, 5 My
    1811
  J. E. McCormack and Lucinda O. Mason,
    30 N 1856

Births:
  Page one.
    David Mason, 4 S 1789
    Barbara Mason, 5 Oc 1794
      Died 27 S 1873 [No entry appears showing whose death date is given]
  Page two.
    George Mason, 19 Je 1812
    Jonathan Mason, 12 N 1813
    Simon Mason, 16 Ap 1815
    Peter Mason, 19 Ja 1817
    Amos Mason, 22 S 1818
    Solomon Mason, 25 Ag 1820
    Lidyann Mason, 25 N 1822
    Andrew Mason, 10 My 1824
    Julia Ann Mason, 8 Ap 1826
  Page three
    J. E. McCormack, 19 F 1827 [19 over 27]
    Lucinda McCormack, 7 Jl 1839
    Emma McCormack, 5 Ag 1858
    Laura McCormack, 1 N 1859
    Hardy McCormack, 24 My 1861
    Ira McCormack, 25 Ja 1863
    E. J. McCormack, 5 D 1866
    Fred McCormack, 22 My 1876
  Page four
    Joshua Mason, 28 S 1828
    Elizabeth Mason, 7 Ja 1830
    Dillon B. Mason, 15 D 1832
    Caleb W. Mason, 8 Ja 1834
    Lucinda A. Mason, 7 Jl 1839
    Barbara Mason, d/of Simon Mason, 13 Ja 1850
Deaths:
  Barbara Mason, 15 F 1873
  Amos Mason, 20 Ap 1823
  Lidyann Mason, 30 Ap 1823
  Julia Ann Mason, 10 Ag 1873
  Elizabeth Mason, 25 Oc 1834
Note:
  Museum Card: This is the Ella Tycer Bible given to Florence Landore by Ella...

MORRIS FAMILY RECORD

Surnames
  Cooke   Morris
  Davidson   Porter
  Dinwiddle
Places
  Eugene, OR

THE HOLY BIBLE. New York: American Bible Society, 1848. VH, VWI: Linn County Museum. Brownsville, Oregon.

Inscription:
  Property of H. E. Morris. Eugene, Oregon July 25, 1934. George J. Morris
Marriages:
  George Jackson Morris and Elizanna Matilda Cooke, 13 F 1844
  William Montgomery Davidson and Sarah Rosetta Morris, 2 Je 1867
 Births: Page 1
  George Jackson Morris, 15 Mr 1818
  Elizanna Matilda Morris, 6 Ja 1825
  Joseph Henry Morris, 15 Mr 1845
  Sarah Rosetta Morris, 24 Oc 1848
  Augustus Corandin Morris, 14 Jan 1852
  Mary Humphrey [remainder of entry obliterated]
  Mary Humphrey Morris, 27 Ap 1855
  Addie Longdon Morris, 14 Oc 1858
  Charles Leander Morris, 25 Ag 1861
  Harlie Everett Morris, 5 Je 1864
  Irene Eveline Morris, 2m F 1864
Births: Page 2.
  Repeats page one except:
    Elizanna Matilda Cooke, 6 Ja 1825

Deaths: Page 1.
  Augustus Corandin Morris, 4 S 1853, aged 1 year 7 mo and 21 days
  Joseph Henry Morris, 19 Jl 1896 aged 51 years 4 mo and 4 days
  George Jackson Morris, 2 Ag 1896, aged 78 years 4 mo and 17 days
  Elizanna Matilda Cooke Morris, 9 Ja 1903 aged 78 years and 3 days
  Charles Leander Morris, 15 May 1924 aged 62 years 9 mo and 10 days
  Minnie Humphrey Morris Dinwiddle, 14 Jl 1922 aged 67 years 2 mo and 17 days
Deaths: Page 2.
  Addie Longdon Morris, 14 N 1914 aged 56 years 16 days
  Sarah Rosette Morris Davidson, 17 F 1928 aged 79 years 3 mo 23 days
  Irene Eveline Morris Porter, 20 N 1940 aged 73 years 9 mo and 18 days
  Harley Everett Morris, 5 Ag 1946 aged 82 years 2 mo

****

McKINNEY FAMILY RECORD

****

Surnames
  Keshlear   McKinney

[Title page missing, New Testament title page Cooperstown, N.Y.: H. & E. Phinney, 1828.] 1-H, VWI: Linn County Museum. Brownsville, Oregon.

Births:
  John McKinney, 3 Ap 1798
  William M. McKinney, 20 Ag 1820
  Wilson S. McKinney, 16 Oc 1823
  Matilda Ann McKinney, 11 D 1825

Zerrelda G. McKinney, 13 F 1827 [27 over 22]
  Elizabeth McKinney, 12 Je 1830
  John F. McKinney, 13 Je 1832
  Joseph A. McKinney, 7 Ap 1835
  Sarah R. McKinney, 1 Ag 18-- [page torn]
  Jacob K (?)eshlear, 12 F 1818
  George B. McKinney, 27 Jl 1840
    [Remainder of page torn and illegible]
Deaths:
  Sarah R. McKinney, 28 S 1843
  Wilson McKinney, 2? Je 1844
  Ann ----ney, 1847
    [Remainder of page torn]

****

ROBERTSON FAMILY RECORD

****

Surnames
  Hewitt   Robertson
  Lunn   Snell
  Mitchell
Places
  High River, Alba   Mongolia, Ont.
  Goodwood, Ont.

Inscription:
  John Hewett, Goodwood, Ont.
  Robert H. Robertson. Mongolia, Ont. Jany 23, 1883
  R. H. Robertson. High River, Alba. March 15th 1/96
  Elizabeth Mitchell from her departed Aunt E. Lunn.
Marriages:
  John Hewitt to Elizabeth Mitchell, 23 F 1871
  Robert Henry Robertson to Emma Jane Snell, 21 N 1883

To:
  Elizabeth Lunn
  Elizabeth Mitchell
  John Hewitt
  John Frederick William Hewitt
  Sarah Selina Elizabeth Hewitt
  Robert Henry Robertson
  Emma Jane Snell
Births:
  [Dates were not associated with any names.]
  August 2, 1802
  June 6, 1848
  Aug. 28, 1844
  March 3, 1872
  March 3, 1872
  Sept. 7 1857 RHR
  Dec. 1, 1863
Deaths:
  Elizabeth Lunn, 1 Ag 1865 aged 63 years
  Elizabeth Hewitt, 9 Mr 1872 aged 23 years
  Emma Jane Robertson, 15 Ap 1833

****

SMITH FAMILY RECORD

****

Surnames
  Brenner   Habersham
  Brunner   Little
  Frisby   Martin
  Githen   Smith
Places
  Albany
  Linn Co.   Pine Grove
  Peoria   Santa Barbara, CA
                       Seattle, Wa

Holy Bible. Philadelphia: William W. Harding, 1872. VH, VWI: Linn County Museum. Brownsville, Oregon.

Marriages:
Left Column
  James P. Smith and Sarah Martin, 7 F 1856
  Lenetta J. Smith and Frank Frisby, 9 Mr 1881
  M. E. Smith and R. P. Habersham, 14 F 1888
  Sheridan Smith and Nellie Githen, 19 F 1896
Right Column
  John Smith and Susannah Little, 27 Mr 1794
Births:
Page one. Left Column
  Mary Adeline Smith, 15 Oc 1856
  Lenetta Jane Smith, 13 Je 1859
  Martha Eveline Smith, 23 My 1862
  Nancy Elizabeth Smith, 5 Oc 1864
  Charles Sheridan Smith, 9 F 1867
  James N. Smith, 24 Jl 1811
  Sarah Martin, 22 Ag 1834
Page two. Right Column
  Nancy Smith, 12 D 1794
  Mary Smith, 11 N 1796
  Jane Smith, 30 Ja 1799
  Robert Smith, 15 Jl 1801
  John Little Smith, 23 Oc 1803
  Elizabeth Smith, 11 F 1806
  Ruth Allen Smith, 11 Oc 1808
  James Newton Smith, 24 Jl 1811
  Margaret Smith, 23 Ap 1814
Page two Left Column
  Bessie Laura Frisby, 30 N 1884
  Stephen Smith Habersham, 7 Mr 1891
  Mary [Laura crossed out] Francis Frisby, 22 F 1892 [22 written over 24]
  Frank Leo Smith, 27 S 1897
  Grace E. Smith, 17 Ag 1901
Deaths:
Page 1
  Mary Adeline Smith, 3 D 1863 aged 7y 1m 18days
  James Newton Smith, 18 D 1889
  Sarah Martin Smith, 10 D 1917
  Nancey Elizabeth Smith, 16 D 1931
  Lenetta Frisby, 16 Ap 1932
  Martha Eveline Habersham, 11 D 1928
  Charles Sheridan Smith, 16 N 1934

Frank L. Smith, 20 My 1965
Mary Liska Smith, w/of Frank Smith, 10/3/79 age 84

Page 2
Robert Smith, 21 Ap 1825
Elizabeth Smith, 2 Ag 1825
Susanah Smith, 5 N 1830
John Little Smith, 30 D 1830
John Smith, Sen., 9 Je 1832
Ruth A. McD [Smith crossed out McD----- written over], 6 F 1884
Nancy Martin, 28 Mr 1884
James Newton Smith, 18 D 1889, 78 yrs 4 ms 24 days

Obituaries:

Charles Sheridan Smith, aged 67 years, passed away at the donation land claim on which he was born, in the Peoria community, on Friday, Nov. 16th... His parents James N. and Sarah Martin Smith, were early pioneers of Linn County.

He is survived by one daughter, Mrs. Arnold Brunner, Santa Barbara, California, and one son, F. L. Smith, residing near Peoria and other relatives. Funeral in Pine Grove Church, Linn Co... United Presbyterian Church... Pine Grove Cemetery. [Date written on margin, 1934]

Frank L. Smith, 68... Albany... born Sept. 27, 1896 in Peoria moving to Albany in 1938.

Surviving is his widow, Mary Liska Smith, whom he married March 27, 1920 in Seattle, Wash. Also surviving is a sister, Mrs. Grace Brenner, Santa Barbara, CA.

Oakville United Presbyterian Church. Burial Twin Oaks Memorial Gardens.

****

FINLEY FAMILY RECORD

****

Surnames
  Crawford   Pell
  Finley   Ribilen
  Henry   Price
  Kirk

[Title page missing from Bible.] VH, VWI: Linn County Museum. Brownsville, Oregon.

Marriages:
  Richard C. Finley and Polly Ann Kirk, 18 D 1841
Births:
  Richard C. Finley, 5 My 1814
  Polly Ann Finley, 29 Ag 1827

Children:
  Sarah Ann, 15 May 1843
  Elizabeth, 26 S 1844
  Martha, 2 Mr 1848
  Eliza, 18 Ap 1850
  Nancy, 16 Je 1852
  William B., 17 Ap 1854
  Cyrus V., 1 Ap 1856
  Edna M., 18 Ap 1861
  Amanda Jamima, 30 S 1857
  Alexander K [K over C], 12 Je 1859
  George, 11 S 1864

  George Finley's children
    Althea Beatrice, 23 Je 1891
    Mamie Ruth, 23 F 1893
    Richard Norval, 6 Jl 1894
    Lola Nancy, 17 Je 1897
    Maud Ina, 5 Mr 1899, Sun.
    Georgia Augusta, 22 Ja 1904, Fri.

Deaths:
  Richard C. Finley, 5 Ag 1892
  Polly Ann (Mother), 3 Mr 1866
  Amanda Jamima, 18 Ag 1858
  Cyrus V., 31 Ag 1861
  Martha Finley Price, [nd]
  Sarah Ann Ribilen [nd]
  Elizabeth Crawford [nd]
  Nancy Pell, D 1929
  Enda Marian Henry, 12 Je 1930
  George, 2 Oc 1944

****

WILEY FAMILY RECORD

****

Surnames
  Campbell   Wiley

HOLY BIBLE. New York: American Bible Society, 1869. VH, VWI: Linn County Museum. Brownsville, Oregon.

Inscription:
    July the 23, 1872 James M. Wiley his book. Price 60 cents This book given to Naomi Elizabeth Wiley by her father, J. M. Wiley, 25 D 1927

    Elizann Wiley Sarah
    A. Campbell
Births:
  John M. Wiley, 10 N 1812
  Eliza A. Wiley, 6 A(?) 1818
  Avaline Wiley, 15 Ja 1837
  Mary J. Wiley, 7 Je 1838
  Eliza Wiley, 1 Mr 1841
  Isaac Wiley, 26 F 1843
  Sarah A. Wiley, 21 Mr 1845
  Maria L. Wiley, 4 Mr 1849
  John P. Wiley, 16 N 1851

James M. Wiley, 16 Ag 1861
Eliza A. Wiley, 16 Ag 1818
Deaths:
Sarah A. Campbell, 17 Ag 1881
John M. Wiley, murdered, 19 Oc 1862
Avaline Wiley, 1 Ap 1868
Mary Jane Wiley, 28 F 1858
John P. Wily, 3 Mr 1858
Eliza A. Wiley, 29 Ap 1877

Sarah A. Campbell, 17 Ag 1881

****

WILEY FAMILY RECORD

****

Surnames
  Gilbert   Wiley
  Higgins
Places
  Sweet Home, OR   Linn Co., OR

THE HOLY BIBLE. New York: American Bible Society, 1852. 1-H, VWI: East Linn Museum. Sweet Home, Oregon.

Marriages:
Andrew Wiley and Lucy Wiley, 14 N 1843
Births:
Page one.
  Andrew Wiley, 17 N 1819
  Lucy Wiley, 14 F 1820

  Mary Emaline Wiley, 28 Ag 1846 [Jl crossed out Ag inserted]
  Charles Taylor Wiley, 14 Ap 1848
  Amanda Jane Wiley, 19 Jl 1851 [Ag crossed out Jl inserted]
  Elizabeth Ann Wiley, 26 Jl 1854
  Susan Wiley, 14 Oc 1856
  George Wiley, 20 Oc 1858

        Robrt Wiley, 15 N 1860
        Lilly C. Wiley, 13 Jl 1866
Page two.
[Birth and marriage information is repeated
    as above with the following changes:]
    Andrew Wiley and Lucy Higgins, 14 N 1843
    Mary Emeline Wiley, 20 Ag 1846
    Amanda Jane Wiley, 19 Jl 1854
    Harriet E. Wiley, 19 Je 1868
Deaths:
    Charles Taylor Wiley, 16 Ag 1852
    Lucy Wiley, 20 Ag 1864
Obituary:
    Died 25 Ja 1890 at Sweet Home, Linn Co.,
    OR. Dr. J. N. Gilbert

****

MOSS FAMILY RECORD

****

Surnames
    Barr   Moss
    Cecil   Poley
    Dewey
Places
    Linn Co., OR

THE HOLY BIBLE. Hartford: Case, Lockwood &
    Co., 1866. VH, VWI: East Linn Museum.
    Sweet Home, Oregon.

Marriage Certificate:
    Zealey B. Moss and Emaline Barr was
    married Feb. the 16th 1862 by H. B.
    Poley. J.P., Linn Co., Oregon
Births:
    Mary Elvira Moss, 30 Ag 1863
    Harriett Elmira Moss, 30 Ap 1865
    Lydia Ann Moss, 8 Ag 1867
    William Mack Moss, 27 Je 1870
    Orta Custus Moss, 22 Ap 1872

Infant babe, 1 F 1874
Anie Orlena Moss, 26 Ag 1875
Henrietta Grace, 23 Mr 1878
Lola Maud, 9 My 1880
Stephen Jesey Moss, 25 My 1882
Zelly Bradley Moss, 29 My 1884
Ladona Francis Moss, 12 Ja 1891 [91 over 90]

Deaths:
Z. B. Moss, 25 My 1893
Emeline Moss, 11 S 1919
Anna Dewey, 4 Je 1923
Mary Alvira Cecil, 25 My 194-

****

HAMILTON FAMILY RECORD

****

Surnames
  Barr   Hand
  Bryant   Larsen
  Crain   Mealey
  Crane   Moss
  Dickinson   Nichols
  Edwards   Rice
  Ferry   Ryan
  Hamilton
Places
  Astoria   St. Clair Co., MO
  Massachusetts

THE HOLY BIBLE. [Title page information not available]

Inscription:
  Father and Mother from William and Fannie, Christmas 1903

Marriage Certificate:
  This certifies that Asher Ferry Hamilton of St. Clair Co., Missouri and Mary Elizabeth Crane of St. Clair Co.,

Missouri were joined together by me in the Bonds of Holy Matrimony at ___ on the 2nd day of March in the year of our Lord 1873. In the presence of Addie Hamilton; Silas Hamilton. Signed: _____

Marriages:
  Lulu Hamilton and Syrus V. Barr, 22 Oc 1891
  Fannie Hamilton and William R. Mealey, Ag 1901
  Charlie Hamilton and Betty Edwards, 19 S 1898
  William Hamilton and Fannie Bryant after her death he married Thora Larsen of Astoria
  Ruth Hamilton and William Hand, 7 D 1904
  Jennie Hamilton and Cliff G. Rice, 5 Oc 1904
  Bessie Hamilton and Will Dickinson after his death she married James Ryan ex-service man of World War I
  Harley James Hamilton and Gladys Moss, 2 Jl 1915

Births:
  Olive Lulu Hamilton, 31 Ja 1874 [31 over 11]
  Fannie Rachel Hamilton, 31 Ja 1876
  Charles Asher Hamilton, 30 Mr 1878 [78 over 80]
  William Silas Hamilton, 1 Oc 1880
  Ruth May Hamilton, 10 Jl 1883
  Jennie Mabel Hamilton, 28 Jl 1887
  Bessie Pearl Hamilton, 22 Mr 1890
  James Harley Hamilton, 27 Jl 1892
  Andana Hamilton, 7 My 1825

Deaths:
  Asher Ferry Hamilton, 3 Oc 1913, age 68
  Fannie Rachel Hamilton Mealey, 17 F 1917 age 41
  Ruth Hamilton Hand, 21 Je 1933 age 49 [49 over 44]
  Mary Elizabeth Hamilton, 7 Jl ----, age 88
  Andana Hamilton, 14 S 1914

Memoranda:
  James L. Crain born 29 N 1825
  Rachel A. Crain born 21 Je 1835

Mary E. Crain born 22 Oc 1852
Asher Ferry Hamilton born 16 D 1845
Untitled page:
 Aseneth Nichols mother of Andana Hamilton born in Massachusetts
 Asher Ferry father of Andana Hamilton born in Massachusetts

****

MURPHY FAMILY RECORD

****

Surnames
  Holleman   Robinett
  Murphy
Places
  Dorris Bridge, CA   Knox Co., IL
  Jackson Co., OR   Linn Co., OR
  Jacksonville, OR   Noble Co., CA

HOLY BIBLE. Philadelphia: Jesper Harding & Son, 1858. VH, VWI: East Linn Museum. Sweet Home, Oregon.

Inscription:
 Morvan D. Murphy's book bought February 1st A.D. 1873 at a Sale in Jacksonville, Jackson County, Oregon. Price $2.75
Marriages:
 Morvan Dudley Murphy and Mary Isabell Robinett was married November 4th 1875 at the town of Dorris Bridge, Noble County, California by J. Holleman, County Judge.
Births:
 Morvan D. Murphy, 6 N 1845, Knox Co., IL
 Mary I. Murphy, 22 Ap 1857, Linn Co., OR
 Otto Murphy, 8 Mr 1877, Linn Co., OR
 Infant daughter, 30 Ag 1878, Linn Co., OR
 Infant son, 11 Ag 1879, Linn Co., OR
 Hulda May Murphy, 28 S 1880, Linn Co., OR
 Infant son, 18 Ap 1883, Linn Co., OR

Infant son, 2 Je 1885, Linn Co., OR
Ivan O. Murphy, 7 N 1889, Linn Co., OR

****

HANSEN FAMILY RECORD

****

Surnames
  Bieck   Landgruf
  Dite   Rummel
  Hansen
Places
  Jeff. Co., WI   Rome, WI

[Title page missing. New Testament shows Light of the World as publisher with the revised version issued A.D. 1881.] 1-H, 1-WI: East Linn Museum. Sweet Home, Oregon.

Marriage Certificate:
  This certificates that the rite of Holy Matrimony was celebrated between John Hansen of Rome, Jeff. Co., Wis. and Clara Bieck of Rome Jeff. Co. Wis. on Feb. 24, 1887 at Rome, Wis. by Ferdinand Dite. Witnesses: Albert Bieck, Mary Rummel, Albert Landgruf, Lydia Bieck

****

STEWART FAMILY RECORD

****

Surnames
  Bell   Brown
  Bischof   Fairchilds

Hampton Terhune
Stewart
Places
  Camp Pike, AR   Nebraska City, NB
  Des Moines, IA

HOLY BIBLE New York: American Bible Society, 1856 1-H, 1-WI: Horner Museum. Corvallis, OR

Inscription-Front Cover
  Mr. Ira Stewart and Miss Arafura Bell were united in marriage on the 31st day of July 1918.

  Ira Stewart entered the service of the Gov't as a private soldier on the 10th day of September 1918.

Inscription-Back Cover
  List of names:
    f-llie Terhune
    Mrs. Arafura Stewart
    Mr. Ira Stewart
    Mrs. Ethel Brown
    Mrs. Bell Hampton

  Mr. Ira Stewart and Miss Arafura Bell were united in marriage at Nebraska City, Nebr on the 31st day of July 1918 at the court house, by Judge A. A. Bischof. Witnesses were Robert Stewart and Mrs. Ethel Brown.

  Mr. Ira Stewart left for war duty at Camp Pike, Arkansas on the 10th day of Sept. 1918. Received his honorable discharge on the 13th day of December 1918.

  John Brown died on the 31st day of Nov. 1918 at the county hospital. Sent his body to Des Moines, Iowa for burial to his mother, Mrs. Amanda Brown on the 5th day of December 1918.

My grandmother died on September 8, 1919 between 7 and 8 o'clock on a Monday evening and was buried on a Wednesday afternoon at 2:30 O'clock. Services at St. Mary's Episcopal Church officiated by Rev. Roy Fairchilds. Burial at Warkey cemetery.

[The family register pages had been removed from the Bible]

****

STRAHLEM FAMILY RECORD

****

Surnames
  Everett   Strahlem
  Seitz

SELF-INTERPRETING HOLY BIBLE. New York: John, Fry & Co., [nd]. VH, VWI: Horner Museum. Corvallis, Oregon.

Marriages:
  Wm L. Strahlem and Mary E. Seitz, 26 Oc 1882
  Hattie Belle Strahlem and Willis L. Everett, 14 S 1911
Births:
  Wm L. Strahlem, 26 F 1857
  Mary E. Seitz, 24 S 1860
  Francis W. Strahlem, 11 Je 1883
  Hattie Belle Strahlem, 26 Ja 1888
  George Brinton Strahlem, 13 S 1895
Deaths:
  Wm L. Strahlem, 29 D 1936
  Mary E. Seitz, 15 Ag 1949
  Francis W. Strahlem, 8 S 1884
  Hattie Belle Strahlem, 14 N 1969
  George Brinton Strahlem, 13 S 1961
Stamped front cover:
  From Mother to W. L. Strahlem

****

HARRIS FAMILY RECORD

****

Surnames
  Butler
  Claggett
  Clare
  Finical
  Fower
  Harris
  Henkle
  Henkler
  Hodgin
  Norton
  Ramsey
  Robinson
  Stanley
  Wilson
  Young

Place names
  Fitzgerald, GA
  Grand Island, NB
  Monmouth, OR
  Polk Co., OR
  Red Bluff, CA
  Rutland, FL

THE HOLY BIBLE. New York: American Bible Society, 1881. VH, VWI: The Heritage Museum. Independence, Oregon.

Inscription:
  Mary I. Harris Monmouth, Oregon

Marriage certificate:
  [loose paper stapled to family record pages] [Certificate issued by the County Clerk of the County of Polk dated June 24th AD 1879. That on 26 day of June 1879 at the house of W. L.Hodgin. I, a minister of the Gospel did join in Lawful Wedlock Miss M. H. Harris of the county of Polk and State of Oregon, and E. T. Henkler of the county of Polk, and State of Oregon with their mutual assent. Witnesses; Eli Young, Sarah Claggett. D. T. Stanley, Minister of the Gospel.

Marriages: Left Column
  Samuel Finical and Harriet B. Ramsey, 6 N 1828
  Geo. C. Harris and Mary Jane Finical, 9 N 1852

Harvey S. Norton and Sarah Ann Finical, 15 Je 1858

Marriages: Right Column
Zebadiah Henkle and Mary Bell Wilson, 18 Je 1835 [July 29th 1817 crossed out]
Eli T. Henkle and Margaret Hattie Harris, 26 Je 1879

Jay B. V. Butler and Mary Francis Harris, 31 Mr 1885
Geo. W. Harris and Hattie Fower, 27 F 1887

Births: Left Column
Samuel Finical, 11 Ag 1797
Harriet B. Ramsey, 16 F 1811
Mary Jane Finical, 12 Ap 1830
Sarah Ann Finical, 7 F 1833
Beng-Franklin Finical, 25 N 1835
Harriet Ellinor Finical, 5 Ja 1842
Charles Austin Finical, 9 Je 1844
William Harrison Finical, 12 Oc 1846

Births: Right Column
Geo C. Harris, 19 Je 1811
M. J. Finical, 12 Ap 1830
Margaret Hattie Harris, 23 Je 1855
Geo. Washington Harris, 18 F 1858
Mary Francis Harris, 27 S 1860
Harry Clay Harris, 5 D 1862
Caroline Lee Harris, 4 Jl 1866
Thomas Fredric Harris, 11 Ag 1873

Page two
Births: Left Column
Zebadiah Henkle, 26 Oc 1812
Mary Isabell Wilson, 8 Je 1817 [written over by July 29th 1817, this in different hand and pen]
Eli T. Henkle, 17 N 1846
M. Hattie Harris Henkle, 23 Je 1855
Hermen Claud Henkle, 21 Ag 1880
Ada Mary Henkle, 10 Oc 1884
Ethel Hattie Henkle, 11 Jl 1887
Emma Francis Henkle, 1 S 1890
Herbert Harris Henkle, 5 Ja 1896

Births: Right Column
Abram Henkle, 7 N 1785
Mary Harper Henkle 29 S 1784

Deaths
  Abram Henkle, 7 Ap 1873
  Mary Harper Henkle, 7 Ap 1882
Deaths: Left Column
  Samuel Finical, 31 N 1861
  Harriet Ellinor Finical, 14 N 1842
  Harriet B. Finical, 20 D 1889
  Geo. C. Harris, 19 Je 1886
  M. J. Finical Harris, 15 Je 1892

  Carrie Lee Harris, 21 Ja 1877
  Harry Clay Harris, 8 My 1895
  Sarah Ann Finical Norton, 26 D 1906
Deaths: Right Column
  Zebadiah Henkle, 26 S 1873
  Mary J. Henkle, 18 Jl 1896
  Hermen Claud Henkle, 21 S 1883
  Ada Mary Henkle, 10 Oc 1884
  Ethel Hattie Henkle, 15 Je 1893
  Herbert Harris Henkle, 5 Ja 1896
  Eli T. Henkle, 14 D 1915
  Margaret Hattie Henkle, 5 Je 1920
  Emma Francis Henkle, 9 S 1975
Loose leaf notebook page:
  Addresses:
    Mrs. H. S. Norton, Soldiers & Sailors
      Home, Grand Island, Nebraska
    Miss M. A. Robinson, Rutland, Florida
    William Finical, Red Bluff, Cal.
    B. F. Finical, Fitzgerald, GA
    Mrs. Sidney Clare

Loose leaf notebook page:
Marriages:
  Red Bl-----
  Samuel Finical and Harriet B. Ramsey, 6 N
    1828
  Geo. C. Harris and Mary Jane Finical, 9
    N 1852
  Harvey S. Norton and Sarah Ann Finical, 15
    Je 1858
Births:
  Samuel Finical, 11 Ag 1797
  Harriet B. Ramsy, 16 F 1811
  Mary Jane Finical, 12 Ap 1830

Sarah Ann Finical, 7 F 1833
Benj-Franklin Finicle, 25 N 1835
Harriet Ellinor Finicle, 5 Ja 1842
Charles Austin Finical, 9 Je 1844
William Harrison Finical, 12 Oc 1846
Deaths:
Samuel Finicel, 31 N 1861
Harriet Ellenor Finicel, 14 N 1872
H. B. Finical, 20 D 1889

****
FERGUSEN FAMILY RECORD
****

Surnames
  Fergusen   Mergatroids
  McGilpin   Wells
Places
  Independence, OR

[No title page. New Testament title page includes the information, revised version A. D. 1881...]. 1-H, VWI: Heritage Museum. Independence, Oregon.

Marriage Certificate:
  Mr. Robert Wells of Indep. [Bride's name erased]

Marriages:
  Mr. W. S. Fergusen and Miss R. S. McGilpin, 3 Jl 1881
Births:
  Wellington Samuel Fergusen, 23 My 1854
  Rosie Sophia McGilpin, 8 Je 1861
  Myrtle Rosie Fergusen, 14 Je 1882
  Rexford Alexander Fergusen, 24 Ag 1884
Notes:
  Written on the Bible page facing New Testament: Elder Mergatroids last sermon preached Sunday April 28, 1889.

BRUNK FAMILY RECORD

Surnames
  Brunk   Lucas
Place names
  Eola, OR   Salem, OR

SELF PRONOUNCING S. S. TEACHERS' COMBINATION BIBLE. J. R. Jones, 1903. 1-H, 1-WI: Brunk House. Monmouth, Oregon.

Inscription:
  To Cliff from Ma & Pa Lucas, March 17th, 1917
Marriage:
  Clifford Lawrence Brunk and Esther Lucas, 10 Oc 1916, Salem, OR
Births:
  Clifford Lawrence Brunk, 17 Mr 1889, Eola, OR
  Esther Lucas, 21 My 1898, Salem, OR

Surnames
  Brunk   Sundborg
  Byers   Waller
  Hartson   Wilson
  McDaniel
Place Names
  Eola, OR   Polk Co., OR
  Independence, OR

PARALLEL BIBLE, THE HOLY BIBLE. St. Louis, MO.: The Christian Publishing Co., 1885. VH, VWI: Brunk House. Monmouth, Oregon.
Marriage Certificate:
  This certifies that Thos. W. Brunk of Eola, Polk Co., Oregon and Clara E. Byers of Independence, Polk Co., Oregon were united by me in the Bonds of Holy Matrimony at A. J. Byers on the forth day

of September in the year of our Lord 1889.
In presence of W. H. McDaniel, A. J.
Wilson. Signed H. M. Waller

Births:
  Daugher, 9 S 1890
  Thomas Earl Brunk, 14 Oc 1891
  Cleo. Ernest Brunk, 7 Ja 1898
  Leland Estill Brunk, 11 Jl 1897
  Clareta Marie Brunk, 12 Mr 1903
  Floreta Loree Brunk, 24 Oc 1905

Deaths:
  Daughter, 14 S 1890
  Thomas Earl Brunk, 14 S 1974
  Cleo Ernest Brunk, 20 Ja 1974
  Leland Estill Brunk, 8 Ag 1965
  Clareta Marie Brunk Sundborg, 4 F 1982
  Floreta Loree Brunk Hartson, 25 Ap 1966

Memoranda - Family immersions:
    Thomas W. Brunk
    Clara E. Brunk
    Thos. Earl Brunk, 28 Ag 1907
    Cleo Ernest Brunk, 9 Je 1907
    Estill L. Brunk, 28 Ag 1907
    Clareta Marie Brunk, 28 Ap 1913
    Floreta Loree Brunk, 28 Ap 1913

****

SMITH FAMILY RECORD

****

Surnames
  Jackson   Smith
  Singleton
Place names
  Portland, OR

HOLY BIBLE. Philadelphia: A. J. Holman & Co., 1874. VH, VWI: Brunk House. Monmouth, Oregon.

Births:
  L. E. Smith, 17 F 1830
  Mrs. M. E. Smith, 1 Ja 1835
  Netty Smith, first daughter, 2 F 1865
  Edward Smith, first son, 13 My 1866
  Dan/Don Smith, 13 Ja 1869
  Lotty Smith, 1 F 1872
  Lura Pope Smith, 13 Je 1876 [6 written over 2. Different ink]
  Gloryl Percival Singleton, 8 Oc 1883, first son age 2m 6d
  Mable Ellen Jackson, 26 Je 1886
Deaths:
  Natty Smith, first daughter of Mary and B. Smith, 21 My 1873 aged 8 yrs 3 mo and 21 days
  Mrs. Mary E. Smith, 5 Ja 1880, age 45 years and 5 days
  Gloryl Percival Singleton, 14 D 1883
  Mrs. Alice Jackson, 18 Ag 1886, age 21 yr
  Mable Ellen Jackson, 27 Ag 1886, age 2 mo
  Lottie Smith, 19 Jl 1888, age 17 yrs & 6 mo. 9 o'clock in the morning at the pest house on a Thursday
Loose paper:
  Letterhead of Northern Pacific Railroad Co., Portland, Oregon. June 18, 1886.
    Mrs. Alice Margrit(n)? Jackson died August 17, 1886. Born August 25, 1865

```
*********************************************
*                                            *
*           FOSTER FAMILY RECORD             *
*                                            *
*   Ed. note: The Foster record which        *
*   follows was found in the Foster Family   *
*   Bible. Inserted in this Bible were       *
*   many loose pages of manuscripts, clip-   *
*   pings, additional Bible pages etc.       *
*   These records have been entered as       *
*   complete family records and referenced   *
*   back to the Foster Bible.                *
*                                            *
*********************************************


        ***************************

                FOSTER FAMILY BIBLE

        ***************************
```

Surnames
  Clark   Klippel
  Currier   Lewis
  Ewing   McDowel
  Foster   Mercer
  Hartin   Mills
  Hay   Schminck
  Hoy   Sellers
  Hubbard   Smith
  Humphrey   Walters
Places
  Benton Co.   Missouri
  Coshocton Co., OH   Vermont

THE HOLY BIBLE. George Lane and Levi Scott, 1850. VH, VWI: Schminck Memorial Museum, Lakeview, Oregon.

Inscription:
  Signed, James Foster
Marriage Certificate: [Taped on back cover]
  Coshocton County, Ohio. Andrew Foster to Elizabeth Smith, State of Ohio, Coshocton

County, 33. I hereby certify that on the 22nd day of January I joined together in the Holy State of Matrimony Andrew Foster and Elizabeth Smith of lawful age. Given under my hand and seal this 2nd day of March 1818. Samuel Clark, Justice of Peace. Page 34-Marriage record A. B. C. 1811-1852

Marriages:
James Foster & Elizabeth B. Currier, 3 N 1848
Frank Lewis & Anna E. Foster, 2 Jl 1882
Fred W. Foster & Ada McDowell, 25 My 1887
John A. Foster & Laura M. Mercer, 19 Je 1890
J. D. Sellers & Luvia S. Foster, 9 Oc 1892
Robert G. Hartin & Eudora Foster, 2 N 1892
J. G. Walters & Aurora A. Foster, 11 Oc 1893
L. P. Klippel & Florence E. Foster, 7 N 1900
D. C. Schminck & A. Lula Foster, 6 F 1901
R.[alph] [alph in different ink] C. Foster & Princess H. Belt Hubbard, 17 N 1903
Carol Myron Ewing & Ruby Faltel Foster (Fred's Daughter), 22 Ja 1911, Sunday noon
James Guy Foster & Maybelle M. Hoy [o over a], 30 A 1911
[Paul Foster Ewing crossed out] & Ellen Mary Mills, 5 Ag 1934
Laura Mabel Mercer & John Foster, 19 Je 1890

Births:
James Foster, 4 Ja 1827
Elizabeth B. Foster, 18 Je 1832
Laurena Foster, 7 N 1849
Jacob Manley Foster, 8 S 1850
John Amsden Foster, 29 D 1851
James Andrew Foster, 15 Ap 1854
Angelina Foster, 25 Mr 1856
William Henry Foster, 4 Ag 1857
Anna Elvira, 9 Ja 1860
Fredrick Warner Foster, 11 Mr 1862
Marion Lee Foster, 15 Ja 1864
Elizabeth Florence Foster, 11 Oc 1865

Andrew Foster, 15 Ja 1789
Elisabeth Foster, 1 N 1800 [1 N written in different ink]
Eudora Foster, 11 S 1871
Ralph Currier Foster, 7 N 1874
Artie Lula Foster, 22 F 1878
James Guy Foster, s/of Fredrick, 23 Mr 1888
Ruby Faltel Foster [Foster written in different ink], d/of Fredrick, 22 Ap 1889
Earl Lawrence [Lawrence written in different ink] Foster, s/of John, 7 Oc 1891
Evan Foster Hartin, s/of Endora, 6 S 1894
Aurora Alice Foster, 17 Ja 1868
Luvey Sophronia Foster, 19 N 1869
Helen E. Walters, 20 D 1895
Harriet A. Walters, 24 S 1899
Carmel Foster, d/of Fredrick, 4 My 1896
Harold U. Foster, s/of Fredrick, 26 F 1898
Dora Allie Klippel, d/of Florence, 20 S 1901
Arthur J. Walters, 9 F 1903
Carl Foster Klippel, s/of Florence, 5 Je 1904
Thomas Belt Foster, 7 Jl 1904
Paul Foster Ewing, s/or Ruby, 25 Oc 1911, Wed. 10 AM
Mary Margaret Ewing, d/of Ruby, 7 Je 1915
John David Ewing, 20 D 1920, 2:10 P.M.
Laura Mabel Mercer, 21 Je 1860

Baptisms:
Elizabeth B. Foster, 15 Jl 1855 in Presbyterian Church
James Foster, early 1800's in United Brethern Church
E. Florence Foster, 25 Oc 1895
John A. Foster, early 1890's Methodist Church
Fredereck Warner Foster, early 1890's, Methodist Church

Deaths:
Laurena Foster, 9 N 1849
Jacob Manley Foster, 9 Oc 1854
Angelina Foster, 6 My 1856

Marion Lee Foster, 17 Ja 1865
William Henry Foster, 11 Oc 1869
Anna Foster [Foster written in different ink] E. Lewis, 1 Ja 1884
Luvina S. Foster Sellers, 7 Jl 1897
Dora Allie Klippel, - Oc 1908
James Foster, 19 D 1909
Eudora F. Hartin, 29 D 1910
Harold Neil Foster, s/of Fredrick, 25 N 1918
Elizabeth B. Foster, 12 Je 1921, 2 A.M. Sunday
Andrew James Foster, 24 Ag 1933
Frederick Warner Foster, 22 Mr 1935
Earl Lawrence Foster, s/of John, 27 Ap 1938
Jeanette Pollock Foster, 1938
John Ausden(?) Foster, 25 Jl 1939
E. Florence Klipper, 26 Je 1941
Andrew Foster, Sr., 16 Je 1865
Elizabeth Foster, 7 N 1870
Ada Foster, w/of Frederick, 22 M 1914, Monday 1:45
Mary Margaret Ewing, d/of Ruby & Carl, 7 F 1930
Carl Myron Ewing, h/of Ruby, 10 Je 1961
Ralph Currier Foster, 1961
Dalpheus Carl Schmink, 4 My 1960
Artie Lula Schminck, 14 Mr 1962
Evan Foster Hartin, s/of Eudora, 1962
Agnes Petzold Klippel,w/of Carl, 4 N 196-
James Guy, 17 Ja 1964
Laura Mabel Mercer Foster, Mrs. John, 22 Ja 1952

Obituaries:
Mrs. James Foster born Vermont 18 Je 1832. Moved to Missouri where her parents died. Sister, Mrs. A. L. Humphrey. Arrived Benton Co. 1846. Married 30 N 1848. Daughter, Mrs. D. C. Schminck. 15 children, seven living: John A., Fred W., Andrew J., Ralph C., Mrs. Florence Klippel, Mrs. Aurora Walters and Mrs. Lulu Schminck. Deceased children: Lorena, J. Manley, Angeline, William H., Annie E., Marion R., Louvia S., and Eudora.

James A. Foster, 19 N 1909. b. 4 Jl 1827 in Coshocton Co., OH only surviving member of 9 and came from Virginia stock and Irish stock. Crossed plains in 1845 with ox team from Missouri.

****

FAMILY OF RALPH CURRIER FOSTER
AND
WIFE PRINCESS
[Recorded on back page of Foster Bible]

****

Surnames
   Foster

Thomas James Belt Foster [James in pencil, Belt crossed out], 7 Jl 1904
Vivian Foster, 20 Ja 1907
Dora Lula Foster, 31 Ja 1910
Leona Foster, 27 Oc 1911
Anna Foster, 3 F 1913
Ross Foster, 9 F 1914

****

CURRIER FAMILY
taped on back cover of Foster Bible

****

Surnames
   Alexander   Spooner
   Currier   Smith
   Gould   White
   Humphrey   Woods
   Hunton
Places
   Benton Co.

Children of Jacob Currier, b. 1787 d. 1845, and Elizabeth Smith, born 1786, died 1844, married 1815
- Sisters of Jacob Manley Currier
- Angeline married Fred Woods and then a man named Gould. Stanley Woods is her son
- Laurena White, had no children
- Mary Alexander
- Louvia Anne Hunton
- Sarah Humphrey married A. L. Humphrey first representative in legislature from Benton County, no children, Sophronia killed when a little girl
- Elvira Spooner
- Elizabeth Foster
- Sarah A. Currier (Sally), 28 Ag 1822, died 19 Oc 1849

****

CURRIER FAMILY
In Foster Bible

****

Surnames
- Currier
- Smith
- Poor

Places
- Benton Co.
- Ipwich, MA
- Brownington, VT
- Orleans Co., VT
- Coshocton Co., OH

John Currier, born 1748, Ipwich, Mass., died 1834 Brownington, VT, married 1 D 1722(?) to Mary Poor

Jacob Currier, s/of John, born 1787, died 1845, married 1815 to Elizabeth Smith, born 1786, died 1844

Jacob Manley Currier, 12 F 1827, Orleans Co. VT, died 22 Ja 1920

Marie Foster Currier, 11 Ap 1833, Coshocton Co., OH, died N 1859, married 1850 Benton Co.
Kate Currier, 7 Jl 1862
Laura Mercer, 21 Je 1860

****

POLLOCK FAMILY
In Foster Bible

****

Surnames
  Kennedy   Pollock
  Olmstead   Waugh
Places
  Callie Co., OH   Gallia Co., OH

John S. Pollock, b. 1861
Bertrice Olmstead, 1876
  Children:
    Hortence Pollock, 1897
    Jeannette Pollock, 1899
John Pollock's mother:
  Elizabeth Ann Kennedy, b. 14 Ag 1828
John Pollock's father:
  Thomas Alan Pollock. Native of Gallia Co., Ohio. Jane Waugh came to Callie [Gallia] Co., 1800 [1st Settler written in pencil] they were married 16 F 1874
Elizabeth Ann Kennedy's Mother:
  Jane Waugh, 8 Oc 1795 died 2 S 1865
Elizabeth Ann Kennedy's father:
  Corneluis Kennedy, 1790 died 3 Jl 1833
Jane Waugh's mother:
  Susan, age 93 died 10 My 1855
Jane Waugh's father:
  George Waugh, age 88 died 8 Mr 1858

"The candlestick belonged to Susan, wife of George Waugh who is John Pollock's Great Grandfather on his mother's side."

```
******************************
```

CHANDLER FAMILY RECORD
In Foster Bible

```
******************************
```

Surname
  Chandler   McKinney
  Hinton   Tucker
  Kinzey   Tullock
Places
  California   Lakeview, OR
  Iowa   Ohio
  Lake Co., OR   Wisconsin

[Ed Note: This record was on a loose sheet that appeared to be a page torn from another Bible.]

Marriages:
  Basailial S. Chandler & Rebecca McKinney, 20 Oc 1851, OH
  William T. Kinzey [Kimzey?] & Mary E. Chandler, 27 F 1877, danced in the Oregon hog Pen ARC
  Armona R. Chandler and Wm Tullock, 7 My 1878, Oregon
  Salmon B. Chandler & Hattie Benefiel, 20 Mr 1882, Lake Co., OR
  Adelia A. Chandler & John W. Tucker, 22 D 1886, Lakeview, OR.
Births:
  Besailial S. Chandler, 25 Oc 1825, OH
  Rebecca McKinney, 3 My 1828, OH
  Salmon R. Chandler, 31 Jl 1852, Wisconsin
  Licentio Adino(?) Chandler, 13 Ja 1854, Wisc.
  Armona Rebecca Chandler, 4 Mr 1856, Wisc.
  Mary Ellen Chandler, 3 F 1859, Wisc.
  James Annis Chandler, 18 Mr 1861, Wisc.
  Adelia Adell Chandler, 25 Mr 1863, Iowa
  Hiton Luse Chandler, 12 Ag 1866, Iowa

Helon Ida Chandler, 17 S 1872, California
Armona K. Tullock [crossed out]

Deaths:
Helen Ida Chandler, 7 Oc 1872, Calif.
Mrs. Armona R. Tullock, 9 N 1898, age 42 years 8 mo 5 da
William Tullock, 18 Ap 1899, age 70 yr 2 mo 21 da
Bazailal S. Chandler, 28 Ja 1908, 80 yr 2 mo 5 da
Rebecca M. Chandler, 15 N 1902, aged 74 yrs 6 mo 12 da
John W. Tucker, 17 N 1928, aged 75 yrs 9 mo 2 da
Mary E. Kinzey, 8 Ja 1911, aged 51 yrs 9 mo 5 da
Adell Adelia Tucker, 8 Mr 1950, age 87 yr 11 mo 17 da

Note:
Spelling on printed copy, Bazelial
Also contained in the Bible is a large collection of additional notes, clippings, and manuscript titled "Family of Claude Hinton among Early Pioneers"

End of material contained in Foster Bible
****

****

BOXALL FAMILY RECORD

****

Surnames
  Boscall   Miller
  Boxall   Schminck
  Foster   Smith
  Ilplaick   Tyler
  McCluer

Places
- Adin, Ca
- Amberly, EN
- Big Valley, CA
- Brighton, EN
- Butte Co., CA
- Carlisle, EN
- Gurety, Gy
- Healdsburge, CA
- Isle of Man
- Lakeview, OR
- Macklenburg, GY
- Modoc Co., CA
- New York City
- Oreville, CA
- Paradise, CA
- San Francisco, CA
- Schwerin, GY
- Sonoma, CA
- Stockton
- Stone Coal Valley, CA
- Summer Lake, OR
- Sussex Co., EN

PICTORIAL FAMILY BIBLE. 1892. VH, VWI: Schminck Memorial Museum. Lakeview, Oregon

Inscription:
  Presented to Phoebe D. Schminck by Hugo Schminck Dec. 25, 1897

Marriage Certificate:
  This is to certify that Hugo Schminck of Adin, Calif. and Phoebe Boxall of Adin, Calif. were united by me in bonds of Holy Matrimony at Stone Coal Valley on Sept. 12, 1875 in presence of Mr. & Mrs. John P. Miller. W. A. McCluer, J.P.

Marriages:
  Mary Jane Smith & James Boxall, 9 S 1852, New York City
  Phoebe D. Boxall & Hugo Schminck, 12 S 1875, Stone Coal Valley, Modoc Co., Calif.
  Katie R. Boxall & Geo. W. Tyler, 8 Ap 1885, Healdsburge, Sonoma Co., Calif.
  Nellie Boxall Chapman & Geo. W. Tyler, Stockton, 20 S 1913
  Anne L. Boxall & James Burke, 29 Je 1886, Paradise, Butte Co., Calif.
  Lulu Foster & Dalpheus Carl Schminck, 6 F 1901, Wed., Summer Lake, Oregon

Births:
  James Boxall (came from Brighton near the Isle of Man, England), 16 Ap 1825, Amberley, England
  Mary Jane Smith [nd], Carlisle, England

Hugo Schminck, 24 Mr 1849, Gurety in Macklenburg, Schwerin, Germamy
Phoebe Dorwena Boxall, 23 N 1855, Butte Co., Cal.
Tristrom Newton Boxall, 31 Mr 1857, Butte Co., Calif.
Mary Jane Boxall, 27 D 1859, Oreville, Butte Co., Calif.
Ellen Francis Boxall, 15 Mr 1861, Oreville, Butte Co., Calif.
Jesse Alvira Boxall, 20 D 1863
Barbra Boxall, 24 Oct 1865, Marysville, Calif.
Katie Ruth Boxall, 11 D 1867, Marysville, Butte Co., Calif
Anne Lora Boxall, 29 Je 1869, Marysville, Butte Co., Calif
Dalpheus Carl Schminck, 3 Jl 1876, Adin, Calif.
Lula Foster, 22 F 1878, Summer Lake, Oregon

Deaths:
Jesse Alvira Boxall, 4 N 1865, age 1 yr 10 mo 16 da
Barbra Boxall, My 1866, age 7 mo, Marysville, Calif.
Mary Jane Boxall, 3 Je 1873, age 41 yrs, Big Valley, Modoc Co., Calif.
James Boxall, 7 Jy ----
Katie Ruth Tyler, 1901
Triston Newton Boxall, Oreville, 1910
Nellie Boxall Tyler, 1 Je 1942, San Francisco, Calif.
Phoebe Dowena Boxall Schminik, 27 Ap 1944, Lakeview, Ore.
Anna Boxall Burke, May 11, Chico 1947

Note:
Birth of James Boscall in a village cald Amberly near Arindel casel brot up in Brighton in the County of Susesc [Sussex], England born April 16, 1825. The family name on his mother side was Ilplaick [Clplaick?].

Katie Ruth Boxall
Tustom

Newton borned 31 March 1857 died in Orevill 1910 age 53, I can't tell the month. father died in Orevall July 7 but I can't tell his age or the year. George & I was married in Stockton Sept. 20, 1913. Hugo died April 2 ...

Hugo Schminck, born 24 Mr 1849, age 61
Phebe Schminck, born 23 N 1855. 54
Dolphues, born 3 Jl 1876, age 34
Lulin Schminck, b. 22 F 1878, age 32
Phoebe & Hugo Schminck married 1875 35 years
Dolphues & Lulu married 6 F 1911 married 9 year

```
*********************************
*                               *
*    H. W. MORRIS COLLECTION    *
*                               *
*********************************
```

The following records were copied from a compilation of notes collected by Mrs. Harnet Moore of Benton County, Oregon in the 1920's. Mrs. Moore was trying to identify individuals who qualified as Oregon pioneers and to identify individuals who qualified for membership in the Daughters of the American Revolution.

After Mrs. Moore's death these notes became the property of her daughter Gwendolyn. Gwendolyn subsequently turned the notes over to Mrs. H. W. Morris who placed them in the Benton County Historical Museum in Philomath, Oregon along with other material of historical interest to Benton County.

Included in some of the material there is a note which reads, "copied and corrected" there is no indication what was corrected or who supplied the information for the corrections.

Apparently, Mrs. Moore added clarifing notes as she copied the records. The comments, which appear to be editorial, were in parenthesis in Mrs. Moore's notes. These have been indicated by the use of (Comp. Note:...) in this compilation. When information other than that found in Mrs. Moore's notes was added to this compilation the addition has been indicated by the use of [Ed. Note:...].

The notebook pages, as found in the museum, were no longer in their original sequence; consequently an attempt was made to reassemble this transcription into an order with the records of a family placed together. The sequence of the notes, as found in the museum, has been shown with the name of the record. 5a and 5b indicates page five, side one; page five, side two. There are also pages missing from the original file, when obvious this missing material is noted in an editorial comment. Some pages were not reproduced. These included material concerning the conduct of the organizations which Mrs. Moore attended.

****

HOLGATE FAMILY RECORDS
[Pages 1a, 1b]

****

Surnames
  Holgate   Watt
  Jesse   York
Places
  Benton Co., OR   Pennsylvania
  Corvallis, OR   Sullivan Co., MO
  Ft. Wrangal, AL   Yamhill Co., OR

Marriages:
  Marraid at the residence of D. M. Jesse' in Yamhill Co., Og'n by Rev. John York. Erastus H. Holgate and Anna V. Watt. Agust 30, 1860.
Births:
  Erastus H., fifth child of James and Sylvania Holgate, 22 Ap 1833, PA
  Anna Violette, twelveth child of John and Mary Watt, 19 My 1840, Sullivan Co., MO
  Willard Watt, first child of Erastus H. and Anna V. Holgate, 29 Je 1861, Yamhill Co., OR
  Arthur Everet, second son of E. H. and Anna V. Holgate, 3 My 1863, Corvallis, Benton, OR
  Harry Langford, third son of E. H. and A. V. Holgate, 21 Ja 1867, Corvallis, Benton Co., OR
  Edwin Thayer Holgate, 16 Jl 1869, Corvallis, OR
  Helen Lucile Holgate, 19 D 1875, Corvallis, OR
  Donald Wallace Holgate, 20 My 1878, Corvallis, OR
Deaths:
  Anna V. Holgate, 23 D 1896, buried 25 D 1896, Corvallis, Benton Co., OR
  Edwin Thayer Holgate lost at sea in Alaska waters near Fort Wrangal - ship Clara Nevada
  Erastus Holgate, 8 Ag 1909, Corvallis, OR

****

REEVES FAMILY RECORD
[Pages 2a 2b 3a 3b 40a]

****

Surnames
  Barclay   Reeves
  Lloyd   Starr

Marriages:
- Thomas D. Reeves, s/of John and Mary Reeves, and Nancy W. Lloyd, d/of John and Nancy Lloyd, 4 Je 1846
- James Barclay and Nancy E. Reeves, 19 Ja 1870

Births:
- Thos. D. Reeves, 6 Mr 1814
- Nancy W. Reeves, d/o John and Nancy Lloyd, 13 Mr 1829
- John L. Reeves, s/of Thos. D. and Nancy W. Reeves, 17 My 1847
- Nancy E. L. Reeves, d/of Thos D. and Nancy W. Reeves, 19 Ja 1851
- Madison C. Reeves, s/of Thos. D. and Nancy W. Reeves, 15 N 1852
- Watson G. Reeves, 15 N 1853
- Eliza Jane Reeves, 2 Jl [?] 1855
- L----isa Reeves, 21 Ap 1856
- Marthy Ann Reeves, 3 N 1858
- Anna Charlotte Reeves, 18 Mr 1860
- John Madison Barclay, 29 D 1871
- Claud Starr, 8 S 1880
- Grace E. Starr, 25 Jl 1887
- Tracy M. Starr, 31 Ag 1890
- Son of James and Mary Barclay, 25 D 1871

Deaths:
- Son of Thos. D. and Nancy W. Reeves was born 9 Jl 1848 and died same day
- Son of Thomas D. and Nancy W. Reeves was born 24 S 1849 and died same day
- Watson G. Reeves, 5 Mr 1854, 9 o'clock
- Daughter of Nancy and Thomas D. Reeves born 3 N 1858 and departed this life 14 Ja 1862
- Son of James and Mary Barclay was born 25 of Dec and depart the life the 15 of F 1871
- Nancy W. Reeves, d/of John and Nancy Lloyd, 5 Jl 1862
- John L. Reeves, s/o Thomas D. and Nancy W. Reeves, 4 F 1867
- Thomas D. Reeves 22 F 1886

****

NEWTON FAMILY RECORD
[4a]

****

Surnames
  Cooper   Newton

Newton family record from Mrs. G. W. Cooper copied from brother's Bible.
Births:
  Abiathar Newton, 8 Ag 1806
  Rachel Newton, 16 Ja 1805
  Heziah Newton, 22 Ja 1828
  Norris P. Newton, 18 Ap 1830
  Isaac H. Newton, 1 Ja 1832
  Cynthia E. Newton, 1 Oc 1833
  Corlista Tamer Newton, 30 Ja 1838
  Gamaliel G. Newton, 7 N 1839 (Pioneer)
  Jasper Newton, 14 Ap 1843
Note: This Bible is in Washington, D.C. copied and corrected

****

COOPER FAMILY RECORD
[5a 5b]

****

Surnames
  Cooper   Junkins
  Evans   Newton
  Hinkle
Places
  Philomath

Inscription:
  Presented to James and Sena A. Cooper, December 25 AD 1887. George W. Cooper
Marriages:
  James Cooper and Sena Ann Evans, d/of Thomas H. and Nancy Evans, 13 Ja 1850

George Washington Cooper and Margaret, d/of G. G. and Susan Newton, 31 Mr 1894

Births:
Jas Cooper, 2 Jl 1824
Sena Ann E. Cooper, 20 F 1830
Thos. H. Cooper, 9 Ja 1851
Nancy A. Cooper, 6 S 1853
Frances Marion Cooper, 7 D 1855
George Washington Cooper, 1 Oc 1858 [19 Mr 1861 crossed out]
Mary Frances Cooper, 19 Mr 1861
Robert E. Cooper, 27 F 1865
Margaret Newton Cooper 7 F 1865
Altha Opal Cooper, 11 S 1896

Deaths:
Frances Marion Cooper, 13 Ap 1891
James Cooper, 20 N 1891
Dr. Robert E. Cooper, 29 My 1896
Sena Ann E. Cooper, 31 D 1909

Note:
Oldest child Jerry Hinkle. Philomath

Cooper Bible of Thos. Cooper at E. G. Newton's. (Evans Bible). Mrs. Junkins. Copied and Corrected.

****

WOOD FAMILY RECORD
[6a 6b]

****

Surnames
  Henkle   Wood
Places
  Appanoose Co., IA   Lee Co., IA
  Benton Co., OR   Oregon Territory

Births:
Susann Wood, 11 S 1840, Lee Co., IA
Amos Wood, 8 Ja 1843, Lee Co., IA
Abraham Wood, 11 Ja 1825, Lee Co., IA
William Wood, 16 Mr 1841, Appance Co.[Appanoose], Iowa
Mahala Wood, 9 My 1849, Appanise Co., IA

Sary Ellen Wood, 28 My 1851, Appanise Co., IA
Martha Wood, 18 N 1854, Oregon Territory, B[enton] Co.
Jesse T. Wood, 24 F 1857, O[regon] T[erritory], B[enton] Co.
Charles Lafayette Wood, 28 Je 1861, B[enton] Co., Oreg.
Abraham Henkle, 7 N 1785
Mary Henkle, 29 S 1784

Deaths:
Abraham Henkle, 7 Ap 1873

****

SCOTT FAMILY RECORD
[8a]

****

Surnames
  Scott
Places
  Walla Walla

Notes:
Avery and Pryor Scott [father crossed out] uncle of next John Scott here in town. His father died on colera on plains left mother and baby at Walla Walla. Pryer married his brother's wife.

****

EVANS FAMILY BIBLE
[8a 8b]

****

Surnames
  Cooper   Evans
Places
  Marion Co.   Sublimity
  Platte Co., MO

THE HOLY BIBLE. Geo Lane & Levi Scott, 1850.

Marriages:
  James Cooper and Seny Ann Elizabeth Evans was married January 13th 1850

Births:
  James Cooper, 2 Jy 1824
  Seny Ann Elizabeth Cooper, d/of Thomas H. and Nancy Evans, 20 F 1830
  Thos. Harrison Cooper, 9 Ja 1851 [6 S 1853 crossed out]
Note:
  Tos. Evans, Mo. Platte Co. Nancy. 52. Married Marion Co. came to Sublimity died

  Jas. Cooper 59 yrs ago

****

EVANS FAMILY RECORD
[11b 12a 12b]

****

Surnames
  Allen   Cooper
  Biddle   Evans
Births:
  Rebecca J. Evans, 11 Ag 1835
  Sarah J. Evans, 22 Ag 1837
  Missouri A. Evans, 25 S 1841
  Mary C. Evans, 17 S 1845
  James O. Allen, 22 Je 1870
  Charley T. Allen, 25 D 1872
  Frances C. Allen, 27 D 1875
  Nancy Ann Cooper, 6 S 1853
  Frances Marion Cooper, 7 D 1855
  George Washington Cooper, 1 Oc 1858
  Mary Frances Cooper, 19 Mr 1861
  Robert E. Cooper, 27 F 1865
  Thomas H. Evans, 7 F 1808
  Nancy Evans, 26 Je 1812
  Robert W. Evans, 3 D 1833 (33 torn)

[Ed Note: The following list of names appears following the account of the Chambers family on page 11b]

Amos Evens
Sarah Jane
Phoebe Ann
Clarinda Gertrude
Geo. Washington killed in accident
Walter Evans
Albert Biddle
2 or three infants

[Ed. Note: The note, "when about 10 years old runaway" appears in margin opposite the names Walter Evans and Albert Biddle. It is not clear to whom the note is refers.]

****

SARAH ANN KISER'S
ACCOUNT OF OVERLAND JOURNEY
[Copied from a record in her handwriting]
[14a 14b 15a 15b]

****

Surnames
  Casner   Kisor
  Freel   Parkinson
  Kiser   Reynolds
Places
  Canesvill   Muscatine Co., IA
  Council Bluffs, IA   Ohio
  Des Moines, IA   Pennsylvania
  Lafayette, IN   Tippecanoe
  Missouri   Warren Co., IA

Grandfather (Comp. Note: Philip) Reynolds
  d. N. 21st (Comp. Note: 1874. Her mother's grandfather, aged 111 yrs.)
Elizabeth M. Kisor died 7 N 1857
John F. Kisor died 30 D 1863

Geo. W. Kisor Jun. died 26 Ag 1865
George W. Kisor Sen died 28 Mr 1896 aged seventy-three years one mo. and one day.
Sarah Ann Kisor died June 23, 1911 aged 82 yrs 1 mo 10 days

Amos Freel and Elizabeth Reynolds was married somewhere in Indiana near Layfayette, I think in Tipcanoe [Tippecanoe] County and lived in Indiana till they had six children, five girls one boy, then they moved to Iowa lived there a number of years. Several years in Muscatine county and then moved to Waren County near Des Moin City lived there till the spring of fifty-two then started for Oregon with his whole family of twelve children and three sons-in-laws. The three oldest daughters being married. The first one, Sarah Ann, married George W. Kisor from Ohio. Sophia, the second daughter, married Johnathan Parkinson from Pencilvania. The 3 one married a man by the name of John Casner from Mosouria. We had to lay by 2 weeks near Canesvill [Ed. note: Kanesville is present day Council Bluffs, Iowa] before we could get across the river. At last they brought a steam boat there to help the people across. Then after we had traveled a day or so Johnathan Parkinson changed his mind and wouldn't go any farther took his wife and 2 children and went back to Cainsvill. This was in April. Wee got along all right until the fifth of June a little Francis Marian took the colery and died (Comp. Note: This was her brother) then the father, mother and 2 daughters and three sons died in eleven days. One of the daughters was Mary Casner, wife of John Casner. She left 2 little boys and husband. The other daughter was Mariah Freel and the little boys names was Francis Marian and Marquis Lafayeth and the babe was Charles Wesley. They all died in eleven days then there was four daughters and one son left. The oldest daughter, Sarah A. Kisor, wife of George W. Kisor and Nancy June Freel and sixteen years old and Elizabeth Lucy and Martha Elan and Ursula and William Jasper four fourteen years old that...

****

KISOR FAMILY HISTORY
Author unknown
[10a 10b 11b]

****

Surnames
 Chambers   Kiser
 Freel   Kisor
Places
 Benton Co., OR   Newport
 Missouri   Philomath, OR
 Monroe, OR   Portland, OR

where they had to stop. When they got here they settled at Portland where Clarinda was born. Some other people were coming to Benton Co. so they decided to come to. 1853 moved and took up the homestead in the Alpine district.

The father (Comp. Note: Geo. W. Kisor) was born in Ohio and became a resident of Indiana, where he was married to Miss Sarah Freel. They joined a party which started across the plains in 1852, the year in which there was a large movement of homeseekers toward the northwest. At this time the cholera was epidemic on the overland route and hundreds of travelers succumbed to the disease. In the number were the father, mother, 3 sisters, and 2 brothers of Mrs. Kiser all of whom died within the period of eleven days. Mr. and Mrs. Kiser reached Portand, Ore. after great suffering, almost miraculousy escaping the many dangers of the long and wearisome journey. After the birth of their daughter Clarinda they moved to

Monroe, Benton Co. and lived there until 1862 when they took up their residence on the location now occupied by Philomath; Mr. Kisor being one of the founders of the town. Miss Kiser grew to womanhood and secured her education in Philomath schools and the college and became acquainted with Prof. Jas. Chambers to whom she was married in 1870. He was a native of Missouri but was reared in Benton Co. coming there in 48. He was educated in Williamette University and afterwards taught in Philomath College. In 1882 he and his wife removed to the Selitz Indian Reservation. Mr. Chambers having been appointed post trader. He died in Aug. 1883 at the age of 37 being the victim of consumption which was brought on following an attack of pneumonia. He served 3 terms as a member of State legislature and annual terms as Co. Com. After the death of her husband Mrs. Chambers was granted a license as post trader by U. S. government and she is the only woman that was ever officially authorized by the govt. to trade with the Indians. She remained most of the time on the reservation until 1910. When she moved to Newport. Mother died Je 23, 1911.

****

HORNING FAMILY
[11a]

****

Surnames
  Horning   Johnson
Places
  Berlin, Germany

F. A. Horning born near Berlin, Germany. Came to Mo. at 4 yrs of age. Born Aug. 10, 1824. Died June 18 1890.

His wife was Mary A. Johnson born Sept 7, 1828. Died Aug. 2 1868.

Both are buried at Crystal Lake Cemetery.

****

BURNETT FAMILY
Captioned Hamen Lewis Family
in Mrs. Moore's notes
[13a 13b]

****

Surnames
  Burnett   Lewis
  Johnson   Mahaffey
  Keesee
Places
  Corvallis, OR   Klamath Co., OR

Deaths:
  Burke Franklin Burnett, 11 Je 1862
  John Curran Burnett, 22 Jl 1877, drowned, "Another link in loves chain is broken" farewell my dear boy. God grant that we may meet again.
  Erma Alice Keesee, 8 Oct 1891, Klamath County, Oregon, our first born loved one farewell
  John Burnett, 1 Mr 1901, Corvallis, OR
  Martha Burnett, 6 Jl 1923, Corvallis, OR., Crystal Lake cemetery
Parents Births:
  Benjamin Franklin Burnett, 6 Ja 1804
  Jane Burnett, 20 My 1808
 Childrens Births:
  Eliza Ann Burnett, 18 F 1828
  Washington Burnett, 28 D 1828
  John Burnett, 4 Jl 1831
  Emaline Burnett, 13 Oc 1833
  Caroline Burnett   25 My 1836
  Joanna Burnett, 15 Ap 1838
  Leoline Burnett, 23 Ap 1840
  George J. Burnett, 5 Ap 1842

Mary Jane Burnett, 30 Mr 1844
Charles C. Burnett, 22 F 1846

Deaths:
Benjamin F. Burnett, 18 Ag 1846
Jane Burnett, 20 F 1853
Eliza Ann Burnett, 20 F 1828
Caroline Burnett, 18 Oc 1836
Joanna Burnett, 12 Oc 1839 [23 Sept. crossed out]
George J. Burnett, 23 S 1844
Mary Jane Burnett, 23 N 1844
Charles C. Burnett, 23 D 1846
Washington Burnett, -- Ag 1863
Loline Burnett, Spring 1868
Emaline Burnett, 14 Ap 1905

Marriages:
Benjamin F. Burnett and Jane Johnson, 17 May 1827
Emaline Burnett and Gabriel B. Mahaffey, 7 D 1859

****

BURNETT FAMILY
[16a 16b]

****

Surnames
  Burnett   Huston
  Callahan   Ingraham
  Hesse   Jones
  Hinton   White
Places
  Amity, OR   Franklin Co., MO
  Corvallis, OR   Pike Co., MO

Marriages:
John Burnett & Martha Hinton, 12 Je 1859 at residence of R. B. Hinton
H. N. Hesse and Emma A. Burnett, 20 Jl 1881 at residence of John Burnett
Ida Burnett and Thomas Callahan, 15 N 1888 at residence of John Burnett
Martha Burnett and Robert H. Huston, 20 N 1889

Ella Ingraham and Bruce J. Burnett, 20 Ja 1903, at residence of R. C. Jones, Amity, Oregon

Births:
John Burnett, 4 Jl 1831, on the bank of the Mississippi in Pike Co., Missouri
Martha Hinton, 28 S 1838, Franklin Co., Missouri
Emma Alice Burnett, 24 Ap 1860
Burke Franklin Burnett, 5 Ag 1861
Ida [Curran, crossed out] Burnett, 25 My 1863
John Curran Burnett, 26 F 1865
Martha Jane Burnett, 1 Je 1867
Brady Frank Burnett, 24 S 1875
John Bruce Burnett, 14 Oc 1878

****

NEWTON FAMILY
[18a 18b]

****

Surnames
  Brown   Newton
  Nash
Places
  Benton Co., OR   Islesboro, ME
  Corvallis, OR

Births:
Rachel Newton, 16 Ja 1805, New York. 1st wife and pioneer mother
Lydia P. Nash [Nash inserted] Newton, 31 Jl 1821, Islesboro, Maine
Deaths:
Sarah Newton, 7(?) Ja 1869
Lovina(?) Newton, 12 F 1873, in infancy
Infant daughter, 26 N 1882, Benton Co. Oreg.
Janie J. Brown, 5 N 1907, Benton Co., Oreg.

Rachel Newton, 18 Ag 1869, Age 64 years 7 months and 2 days
Abrathar V. Newton, 27 Oc 1892, Age 86 yrs, 2 Mo., 19 days
Lydia P. Newton, 3 Ap 1898, 76 yrs, 8 mo, 2 days
Gamaliel G. Newton, 2 Ja 1915, Corvallis, Benton Co., Or., age 75 years 1 mo 25 days
Susan Newton, 17 F 1924, Corvallis, Benton Co., Oregon, age 83 years, 5 mo, 6 days
Note: Copied and corrected

****

NEWTON FAMILY RECORD
[19a 19b 20a 22a]

****

Surnames
  Allen
  Bohannon
  Brown
  Clayton
  Cooper
  Dodge
  Feichter
  Freel
  Garlinghouse
  McCoy
  Newton
  Nots
  Olson
  Whaley
  Wolson
  Wood

Places
  Benton Co., OR
  Canton Co., MA
  Cottonwood, ID
  Hanton Co., MA
  Lee Co., IA
  Licking Co., OH
  Oakesdale, WA
  Philomath, OR
  Whitman Co., WA

HOLY BIBLE. William W. Harding, 1869

Marriages:
  Gamaliel G. Newton and Susann Wood, 26 Oc 1862, Benton Co., Oreg.

George W. Cooper and Margie Newton, 31 Mr 1894, Benton Co., Oreg.
Samuel P. [J.?] McCoy and Dianna Newton, 8 Ag 1896, Oakesdale, Whitman Co., Wash.
George Clayton and Mary E. Newton, 19 Mr 1899, Cottonwood, Idaho
Emery J. Newton and Minnie E. Cooper, 21 Oc 1900, Benton Co., Oregon
Robert Brown and Janey J. Newton, 24 N 1904, Benton Co., Oregon
Alora A. Newton & Pearl Whaley, 18 Dec. 1907, Benton Co.
Robert C. Herron and Cora L. Newton, 12 Oc 1913, B. Co.
Isaac H. Newton and Anna Allen, 26 N 1854
William E. Bohannon and Mahala H. Newton, 19 Ap 1860
Gamahiel G. Newton and Susann Wood, 26 Oc 1862, near Benton Co., near Philomoth
Jasper Newton and Ursula Freel, 9 D 1863
Abrath Newton and Lydia P. Dodge, 2 Ap 1871
Jasper Newton, Wolson, Washington [Ed. Note: May read, " M or W Olson]
Abrathar Newton and Rachel Garlinghouse, 5 Oc 1826
G. W. Betharus and Heziah Newton, 21 Ja 1844
John Feichter and Cynthia E. Newton, 21 Mr 1850
Norris P. Newton & Jistina Nots, 5 S 1853

Births:
Gamaliel G. Newton, 7 N 1839, Licking Co., Ohio
Susan Newton, 11 S 1840, Lee Co., Iowa
Dianna C. Newton, 18 Oc 1863, Benton Co., Oreg.
Margaret Newton, 7 F 1865, B. Co.
Mary E. Newton, 4 Oct. 1866, B. Co.
Sarah Newton, 17 Jan 1869, Benton Co. Oreg.
Lousina (?) Newton, 12 F 1873, Benton Co. Oreg.
Justina Jane Newton, 19 Mr 1874
Alva Abrathar and Emery Jesse Newton, 18 F 1877, B. Co., Oregon

Infant Daughter, 26 N 1882 B. Co.
Cora Lydia Newton, 21 Oc 1883, B. Co. Org.
Abrathar V. Newton, 8 Ag 1806 Hanton
   [Canton] Co., Massachusetts
Mahala H. Newton, 11 Mr 1865
Deaths:
  Corlia Tamor Newton, 5 Ag 1840
  Rachel Newton, 18 Ag 1869
  Isaac H. Newton, 12 My 1874
Note:
  Jasper Newton copied off this record and sent to...

****

PIONEERS
[23b]

****

Surnames
  Abbey   Burnett
  Barclay   Calloway
  Blodgett   Carter
Places
  C. Lake, OR   Clark Co., OH

  Abbey, Edwin A
  Jas Barclay, born 8-4-1828 [came] 50
  Wm Barclay, born 9-19-1805 [came] 50
  Dr. Jas. R. Barclay, born 1819 Clark
     Co., Ohio [came] 50
  Wm Blodgett, 1811 [came] 1847
  John Burnett, 7-4-1831 [came] Ore. 58, C.
     Lake
  Wm Calloway, 1826 [came] Ore 54
  Talbot Carter, 1825 came 1846
  Pete Abbey, father of Edwin A.
  Kitt Abby, brother S-

****

EVANS FAMILY
[25a 25b]

****

Surnames
  Allen   Downing
  Brown   Evans
  Cooper   Lowell
Places
  Corvallis, OR   Sublimity, OR
Births:
  Gracie Lowell, 28 Mr 1886
  George A. Lowell, 26 My 1889
  Arthur G. Allen, 27 Je 1881
Deaths:
  Thomas W. Evans, 14 Ja 1869
  Nancy Evans, 19 Ap 1866
  Robert W. Evans, 9 Ag 1852
  Missoura Ann Downing, 15 N 1865
  Sarah J. Brown, 18 F 1878
  Nancy Cooper Allen, W/of Morris Allen-d/of
    Jas Cooper, 5 Jl 1882, Corvallis
Note:
  Book Thos H. & Nancy, Sublimity, Oregon

****

THE WOOD BIBLE
26a 26b

****

Surnames
  Chenoworth   Henkle
Places
  Champaign Co., OH   Pendleton Co., VA
  Franklin Co., OH   Vermillion Co., IL

Amos Wood was born

Marriages:
 Jesse Wood and Rachel Chenoworth, 4 Oc 1827, Franklin Co., Oh
 (Comp. note: 1st wife. Elizabeth and Joseph their children)
 Jessie Wood and Margaret Henkle, 16 F 1834

Births:
 Jesse Wood, 24 Mr 1804, Penelion [Pendleton] Co., Virginia
 Rachel Chenoworth, 12 D 1803, Franklin Co., OH
 Margaret Henkle, 1 Mr 1815, Penelton Co., Virginia
 Elizabeth Wood, 3 N 1828, Champaign Co., Ohio
 Joseph Wood, 10 Mr 1831, Vermillion Co., Illinoys
 Mary Wood, 16 F 1835, Vermillion Co., Ill
 Phoebe Jane Wood, 24 Ja 1837, V. Co., Ill
 John Wood, 4 My 1838, V. Co., Ill

****

TRIMBLE FAMILY NOTES
28a 28b 29a 29b 30a 30b

****

[Ed Note: Pages 28-30 appear to contain anecdotes about the Trimble family. Much of the material is illegible or written in fragmented notes. The portions which could be deciphered and which contained information which might be of value to a researcher with a knowledge of the people and the area is reprinted. An individual researching this family may wish to examine the original to evaluate the entire record.]

Surnames
- Alex
- Applegate
- Avery
- Brown
- Butterfield
- Dan
- Drum
- Evens
- Fasbest
- Gage
- Hartless
- Henshaw
- McMahon
- Mile
- Moore
- Riglet
- Taylor
- Willson
- Young

Places
- Alsea, OR
- Benton Co., OR
- Boise, ID
- Burnt River
- California
- Chariton, IA
- Colorado
- Coos Bay, OR
- Coquille, OR
- Corvallis
- Devil's Gate
- Green River
- Illinois
- Independence Rock
- Iowa
- Jackson, CA
- Kiger's Isalnd
- Lewisville
- Oregon City, OR
- Pennsylvania
- Roseburg
- St. Joe, MO
- Sheriton
- Washington

D. J. Riglet was in Benton Co. in 53. In 56 sent to Selitz Agency as physician

at Green River.

Samuel T. was buried in Alsea.

Avery, Alex, Butterfield, Young, Gage, Dan --- came in same train. Hartless & Brown... S--- was capt.

67. First man helped cut pine(?) bring to Coos Bay. The wood out & packed the first pack train over it. Came to Benton Co. in 73. Settled in Alsea County. 1905 or 1906 to Corvallis.

He is buried in Alsea in 1919. Born Feb. 11, 1828 past 91 when died, 13 Oct.

Ca[l?] Trimble, Jane Mile in Washington. His two sons married in 78.

Her [Mrs. Even?] father (Trimble) remarried Hulda McMahon. Married in Ia(?). came across in 52. Huron named... Died in Corvallis in 83. Was born in 1776. Was 97 [7 over 6] yrs old buried in Odd Fellows Cemetery. Married in 55 came west. Volunteered & helped .... Ind. up. An Indian captured an old lady and her daugher and was rescued by them. Formed a circle and picked up Mr. fasbest[?] running. They grabbed the women and made off.

Cal met Oregonians in Jackson Col. [Cal.?] came in 62 and went to Grand Round Valley east of Mts. where he married Mary Trimble. Where Ia grounds stands now. Henry Trimble first blacksmith.

Sept. 22-62 married came [here crossed out] Rosburg in 62. 63 came above Boise, Ida. 64 had Mountian fever. Started to Col. [Cal.?] in 64 and goes far as Roseburg. First baby born there in 65 it died. Stayed there till 67. Richard born never was married. Ben born in 36, died Jan 23, 1923, buried in Alsea. Father, Ben, Sortie(?) and Jasper all buried in Alsea cemetery. Took up donation claim on Kigers Island (father) went to Washington in 58 -d and took preemption claim and lived there 50 years. Run off.

Mother[?] died of cancer of jaw and bled to death about 23 May. crossed the Mo River May 1. Sam died in Idaho-cramps. Grandmother Tremble name was Betsy Miller.

Chas Evens crossed plains in 50 came from Iowa to Cal. in 50. Drove a team for Henshaw. Brought a lot of cattle across. Wasn't of age. Crossed back again in 50's. and returned. 56 & 57 or 57 & 58.

Miner in Cal. Serving war when indians -- --- up.

Samuel Trimble crossed the plains. Irish and Welch people born in 1807. Married Nancy Willson. Married in Pa. Moved to Iowa. Grandmother died about 1850. Grandfather was Robert Trimble died in Iowa at age 99 yrs 6 mo. died about 1853 near Sheriton [Ed. Note: Chariton]. Crossed the plains in 48. Captain Will Applegate. Left Penn. moved to Ill. Robt was born there. Benjamin born in Pa. Ed. Trimble born in Iowa Dec. 15, 1842. Jasper born in Iowa. Martha(?) born in 46 and died. Mary Jane born in St. Joe, Mo. Feb. 14, 1848. Went asleep on horse at Burnt River, fell off and broke arm. His mother died on Willow Springs and buried this side of Independence Rock. Robt was buried at Devils Gate on that trip. 4 boys 3 girls. Charlote 2nd child born in Pa. came to Oregan City. Ben & Ed & Father & a young feller named Bill Moore packed horses and went back with supplies leaving 2 boys there.

Came to Benton Co. to Ab Drums place at Lewisville who crossed in 46. They were an aunt and uncle. 9 mo. ---- there traded off and was a blacksmith at Oreg. City ---- of 48 and went to Cal. in 49 & came back in 52. Lottie or Charlotte married Wm Tayler who came in 46 & kept these children.

Father was in Black Hawk war. Brother Ben was in Cayuse War 63 at Rogue River went from there ----- again all -- -- Yellowstone country.

****

KISOR FAMILY
[31a 31b]

****

Surnames
  Campbell   Kisor
  Chambers   Mason
  Freel   Rice
Places
  Benton Co., OR   Corvallis, OR

Geo W. Kisor & Sarah Ann Freel was married 28 Ja 1846
Alex H. Campbell & Sarah Jane Kisor was married 20 Oc 1864
Joshua Mason & Phoebe A. Kisor was married 19 Ja 1869
James Chambers
W. E. Kisor and M. E. Rice was married 10 Oc 1880 at Corvallis, Benton Co. Oregon
Geo. W. Kisor sen. was born 28 F 1823
Sarah Ann Kisor was born 13 May 1829
Amos E. Kisor was born 21 N 1846
Sarah J. Kisor was born 18 Mr 1848
Phoebe A. Kisor was born 4 N 1849
Clarinda L. Kisor was born 13 D 1852
Geo. W. Kisor Jr. was born 10 Mr 1855
Elizabeth A. Kisor was born 21 Ag 1857
William E. Kisor was born 27 N 1858
John L. Kisor was born 19 N 1863
Walter E. Kisor was born 16 Jan 1867
Albert Biddle Kisor was born 19 Dec 1870

****

LLOYD FAMILY
[33a]

****

Surnames
　Burnett　　　　　　　　Jasper
　Cooper　　　　　　　　 Lloyd
　Irvin
Places
　Bultes　　　　　　　　 Philomath
　Mary River　　　　　　 Waitsburg, WA

Mrs. A. H. Lloyd, Waitsburg, Wash. Mrs. Coopers aunt Interpeter for officers in Rogue River War. (86)

Sister of Mrs. Irvin at Philmoth was a Jasper. Settled about Bultes fall 55 Father came in 43. Peter Burnett Capt. of Co. that Mr. ...

Nancy Lloyd named M.R. & M. Peak for her sister Mary who fell in creek as they were crossing in ox team and said this is "Mary River"

****

GOODMAN FAMILY BIBLE
[37a 37b]

****

THE HOLY BIBLE. American Bible Society, 1875.

Surnames
　Craig　　　　　　　　　West
　Goodman

Marriages:
　J. B. Goodman and S. E. Craig, 16 D 1855
Births:
　J. B. Goodman, 15 Mr 1834
　Sarah E. Goodman, 11 Ap 1842
　Martha J. Goodman, 31 Ja 1857
　George W. Goodman, 24 Ja 1859

Olive A. Goodman, 8 Oc 1860
Wm J. Goodman, 22 S 1862
Alice M. Goodman, 25 S 1867
Carie M. Goodman, 19 Ja 1867
Charlie C. Goodman, 24 Ap 1869
Birttie Franklin Goodman, 3 F 1878
Lucy Evey Goodman, 17 Ap 1882
Olive Golda West, 10 Ap 1890
Deaths:
Alice M. Goodman, 24 Oc 1875
Carie M. Goodman, 1 Oc 1875
Olive A. West 28 My 1891
S. E. Goodman (mother) 26 Ja 1894

****

MOBLEY FAMILY RECORD
[38a 38b 39a]

****

Surnames
  Avery   James
  Dan   Klinger
  Gray   Marsh
  Hopkins   Mobley
Places
  California   Missouri
  Holt Co., Mo   Paisley, OR
  Kentucky   Salina Co., MO
  Lake Co., OR   Wilkes-Barr, PA

Marriages:
  William Mobley (Ky) and Caroline Klinger (Penn), 11 Ap 1844

  Punderson Avery (Wilkes-Barre, Penn.) and Elizabeth M. Mobley (Mo.) 13 N 1864

Births:
  William Mobley, 20 Mr 1819
  Caroline Mobley, 19 Ja 1826
  Martha E. Mobley, 12 Ja 1845
  Mary F. Mobley, 3 F 1847

John Mobley, 28 Oc 1848
Robert Mobley, 17 Je 1850
Thomas C. Mobley, 28 Oc 1852
William Mobley, 19 My 1855
Deaths:
John Mobley, 26 Ap 1851
Mrs. Caroline Mobley, 19 My 1855, buried Salina Co. Cal.
Penderson Avery, 22 D 1912
Note: The following not in Bible
Vernoil Ferdinand Hopkins was born 3 Mr 1850
Judson Avery was born Oct 29, 1865
Frankie Avery was born 28 S 1867
Chester P. Avery was born 3 My 1869
Clarence N. Avery was born 24 Je 1872
Martha Caroline Avery was born 1 N 1873
Frankie Avery died 31 Jy 1878
Judson Avery died 23 Ag 1883
Joseph Conant Avery was born 3 N 1875
Grover C. Avery was born 10 N 1883
Virgil B. Avery was born 27 N 1890

Avery geneology is in hands of Florence James, Paisley, Lake Co., Oregon

Averys married in Corvallis, born Holt Co. Mo. crossed plains in 53 to Cal. 58 in Oregon.

Mrs. Edna J. Dan's, wife of Edmund L. Dan's and Daughter of Jr. Gray was born Nov 7, 1867. Died 19 Mr 1889 one daughter, Bertha.

J. C. Avery, 16 Je 1876. Married in 1841 to Miss Martha Marsh

Mrs. Avery 45. Mr. Avery 47. First legislature was held in his log cabin.

****

HAYES FAMILY RECORD
[39]

****

Surnames
  Hayes   Henkle

James Hayes and Caroline C. Henkle was married 20 Oc 1861
James Hayes was born 20 My 1833
Caroline Colestine Henkle was born 15 S 1845
Sarah Olive, first daughter of James and Caroline C. Hayes, was born 10 Ag 1862
Cora Ann Hayes, second daughter of James and Caroline C. Hayes, 29 Mr 1864
Nancy Bell, third daughter of James and Caroline C. Hayes, 9 ...

****

INDEX

****

The index entries refer the reader back to the register of surnames and place names at the head of each Bible record.

ABBEY, 88
Adin, CA, 69
Albany, 40
Albany, OR, 2
Alberta
   High River, 39
ALEX, 91
ALEXANDER, 64
ALKINE, 4
ALKIRE, 4
ALLEN, 78, 86, 89
Alma, 26
Alsea, OR, 91
Amberly, EN, 69
Amity, OR, 84
Appanoose Co., IA, 76
APPLEGATE, 91
Arkansas
   Camp Pike, 51
   Fayetteville, 26
   Pine Knob, 26
   Pope Co., 25
   Prairie Grove, 26
   Van Buren, 25-6
Arkansas Territory, 25
ARMSTRONG, 30
Ashland, 12
Ashland OR, 10
Astoria, 47
AVERY, 91, 96

AVERY, 91, 96
Avoca, IA, 1

BARCLAY, 73, 88
BARKER, 30
BARR, 46-7
BAUTALO, 9
BAWKER, 28
BAXTER, 31
BELKNAP, 12
BELL, 50
Bellfountain, OR, 19
Benton Co., 60, 64-5
Benton Co., OR, 12,
   16-17, 23, 34,
   71-2, 76, 81,
   85-6, 91, 94
Benton Co., OR Terr. 30
Berlin, GY, 82
BIDDLE, 78
BIECK, 50
Big Valley, CA, 69
BISCHOF, 50
BLODGETT, 88
BODINE, 2
BOHANNON, 86
Boise, ID, 91
Boone Co., IN, 10
Boone Co., KY, 17
BOSCALL, 68

BOWKER, 28
BOXAL, 68
BOYD, 19
BRACKEN, 4
BRENNER, 40
Brighton, EN, 69
BROWN, 31, 51, 85-6, 89 91
Brownington, VT, 65
BRUNK, 57
BRYANT, 47
BRYSON, 31
BUCKINGHAM, 19, 34
Bultes, 95
BURKHART, 2
BURNETT, 83-4, 88, 95
Burnt River, 91
BURR, 31
BUTLER, 53
Butler Co., OH, 12
Butte Co., CA, 69
BUTTERFIELD, 91
BYERS, 57

C. Lake, OR, 88
Calapooga, OR, 10
California, 19, 67, 91, 96
  Adin, 69
  Big Valley, 69
  Butte Co., 69
  Dorris Bridge, 49
  Healdsburge, 69
  Jackson, 91
  Kalmath, 12
  Modoc Co., 69
  Noble Co., 49
  Oreville, 69
  Paradise, 69
  Red Bluff, 53
  San Francisco, 69
  Santa Barbara, 40
  Sonoma, 69

California
  Stone Coal Valley, 69
CALLAHAN, 84
Callie Co., OH see Gallia Co., OH
CALLOWAY, 88
Camp Pike, AR, 51
CAMPBELL, 43, 94
Canesville, IA see Council Bluffs, IA
Carlisle, EN, 69
CARTER, 88
CASNER, 79
CECIL, 46
CHAMBERS, 81, 94
Champaign Co., OH, 89
CHANDLER, 67
Chaney Valley, NY, 12
Chariton, IA, 91
CHENOWORTH, 89
CHURCHILL, 4
CLAGGETT, 53
CLARE, 53
CLARK, 16, 60
Clark Co., OH, 88
CLAYTON, 86
COLE, 24
Colorado, 91
COOKE, 37
COOPER, 75, 77-8, 86, 89, 95
Coos Bay, OR, 91
Coquille, OR, 91
Corvallis, 12, 91
Corvallis, OR, 2, 26, 31, 71, 83-5, 89, 94
Coshocton Co., OH, 28, 60, 65
Cottonwood, ID, 86

Council Bluffs, IA, 79
COX, 33
COYLE, 12
CRAIG, 95
CRAIN, 47
CRANE, 47
CRAWFORD, 43
CURRIER, 60, 64-5

DAN, 91, 96
DAVIDSON, 37
DAVIS, 4, 31
Dearborn Co., IN, 17
DeKalb Co., IL, 17
DENNIS, 19
Des Moines, IA, 1, 34, 51, 79
Devil's Gate, 91
DEWEY, 46
DICKINSON, 47
DINWIDDLE, 37
DITE, 50
DODGE, 19, 86
Dorris Bridge, CA, 49
DOHERTY, 9
DOWNING, 89
DRUM, 91
DUCHESS OF KENT, 24

Early, IA, 28
EDWARDS, 47
ELLIOTT, 12
EMMONS, 28
England, 25
  Amberly, 69
  Brighton, 69
  Carlisle, 69
  Sussex Co., 69
Eola, OR, 57
Eugene, OR, 37
Eugene City, OR, 12
EVANS, 75, 77-8, 89
EVENS, 91
EVERETT, 52
EWING, 60

FAIRCHILDS, 51
Farmington, WA, 23
FASBEST, 91
Fayette, OH, 23
Fayette Co., OH, 30
Fayetteville, AR, 26
FEICHTER, 86
FERGUSEN, 56
FERRY, 47
FIECHTER, 16, 31
FINICAL, 53
FINLEY, 43
Fitzgerald, GA, 53
FLETCHER, 19
Florida
  Rutland, 53
FORREST, 19
FOSTER, 2, 60, 64, 68
Fountain Co., IN, 28
FOWER, 53
France
  Paris, 28
FRANK, 9
Franklin Co., MO, 84
Franklin Co., OH, 89
FREEL, 79, 81, 86, 94
FRISBY, 40
FRY, 2
Ft. Wrangal, AL, 72

GAGE, 91
Galle Co., OH see Gallia Co., OH
Gallia Co., OH, 23, 66
GARLINGHOUSE, 86
GEER, 4
GEORGE III (KING), 24
Georgia
  Fitzgerald, 53
Germany
  Berlin, 82
  Gurety, 69

Germany
  Macklenburg, 69
  Schwerin, 69
GILBERT, 12, 45
GITHEN, 40
Glendale, SD, 28
GOBLE, 4
GOODMAN, 95
Goodwood, Ont., 39
GOULD, 40, 64
GRAGG, 30, 34
Granby, MA, 10
Grand Island, NB, 53
GRAY, 96
Great Amer. Desert, 26
Green River, 91
Gurety, GY, 69

HABERSHAM, 40
HAINES, 34
HALEY, 2
HAMILTON, 47
HAMMILL, 28
Hampden Co., MA, 86
HAMPTON, 50
HAND, 47
Hand Co., SD, 28
HANSEN, 50
Hanton Co., MA see Hampden Co., MA
HAPTONSTALL, 23
HARRIS, 4, 53
HARTIN, 60
HARTLESS, 91
HARTSON, 57
HATHAWAY, 1
HAWLEY, 12, 19
HAY, 60
HAYES, 98
Healdsburge, CA, 69
HENDEE, 4
HENKLE, 30, 53, 76, 89, 98
HENKLER, 53
HENRY, 43

HENSHAW, 91
HESSEE, 84
HEWITT, 39
HIGGINS, 45
High River, Alba, 39
Hillsboro, 12
HINKLE, 31, 75
HINTON, 67, 84
HITE, 2
HODGIN, 53
HOEL, 2
HOLDER, 31
HOLGATE, 72
HOLLEMAN, 49
Holt Co., MO, 96
HOPKINS, 96
HORNING, 82
HOWARD, 12
HOWELL, 24, 26
HOY, 60
HUBBARD, 60
HUGHES, 4
HUMPHREY, 60, 64
HUNTER, 2
HUNTON, 64
HUSTON, 84

Idaho
  Boise, 91
Illinois, 4, 19, 91
  Concord, 10
  DeKalb Co., 17
  Iroquois Co., 28
  Jacksonville, 10
  Knox Co., 49
  McLean, 1
  McLean Co., 1
  Morgan Co., 10
  Vermillion Co., 28, 89
ILPLAICK, 68
INGRAHAM, 84
Independence, OR, 56-7
Independence Rock, 91

Indiana, 19, 23
Boone Co., 10
Dearborn Co., 17
Fountain Co., 28
Lafayette, 79
Park Co., 28
Vermillion Co., 28
INGLE, 4
Iowa, 12, 67, 91
Appanoose Co., 76
Avoca, 1
Canesville. see
Council Bluffs
Chariton, 91
Council Bluffs, 79
Des Moines, 1, 34,
51, 79
Early, 28
Lee Co., 76, 86
Muscatine Co., 79
Pottawattamie Co.,
1
Sac Co., 28
Sioux City, 28
Storm Lake, 28
Van Buren Co., 12
Warren Co., 79
Woodbine, 10
Ipwich, MA, 65
Iroquois Co., IL, 28
IRVIN, 95
Isle of Man, 69
Islesboro, ME, 85

JACKSON, 58
Jackson, CA, 91
Jackson Co., OR, 49
Jacksonville, IL, 10
Jacksonville, OR, 49
JAMES, 9, 96
JASPER, 31, 95
Jeff. Co., WI, 50
JESSE, 72
JOHNSON, 16, 31,
82-3
JONES, 84

Josephine Co., OR,
10
Junction City, 12
JUNKIN, 12
JUNKINS, 75

Kanesville, IA, see
Council Bluffs, IA
KENNEDY, 66
Kentucky, 19, 96
Boone Co., 17
KEESEE, 83
KESHLEAR, 38
Kiger's Island, 91
KING, 30
KINZEY, 67
KIRK, 43
KISER, 79, 81
KISOR, 79, 81, 94
Klamath, CA, 12
Klamath Co., OR, 83
KLINGER, 96
KLIPPEL, 60
KNOX, 12
Knox Co., IL, 49

Lafayette, IN, 79
Lake Co., OR, 67, 96
Lakeview, OR, 67, 69
LANDORE, 35
LANDGRUF, 50
LANE, 4
LARSEN, 47
Lebanon, 12
Lee Co., IA, 76, 86
LEWIS, 60, 83
Lewisville, 91
Licking Co., OH, 86
Linn Co., 40
Linn Co., OR, 10,
12, 45-6, 49
LITTLE, 40
LLOYD, 73, 95
LOCHRIDGE, 2
LOWE, 4
LOWELL, 89

LUCAS, 57
LUNN, 39

Macklenburg, GY, 69
MAHAFFEY, 83
Maine
  Islesboro, 85
Marion Co., 77
MARKHAM, 2
MARSH, 96
MARTIN, 40
Mary River, 95
MASON, 35, 94
Massachusetts, 47
  Granby, 10
  Hampden Co., 86
  Hanton Co. see
    Hampden Co.
  Ipwich, 65
MAXWELL, 4
McCAIN, 17, 19
McCLUER, 68
McCONNELL, 25
McCORMACK, 10, 35
McCOY, 23, 86
McDANIEL, 57
McDOWEL, 60
McFARLANCE, 10
McGILPEN, 56
McKINNEY, 38, 67
McKNIGHT, 4, 9
McLAIN, 34
McLean, IL, 1
McLean Co., IL, 1
McMAHON, 91
McREYNOLDS, 4
MEALEY, 47
MERCER, 60
MERGATROIDS, 56
MERRILL, 12
MICHAEL, 16
MILE, 91
MILES, 25-6
MILLER, 68
Miller, SD, 28
MILLRATH, 23

MILLS, 60
MIRES, 19
Missouri, 19, 23,
  60, 79, 81, 96
  Franklin Co., 84
  Holt Co., 96
  Pike Co., 84
  Platte Co., 77
  Salina Co., 96
  St. Clair Co., 47
  St. Joe, 23, 91
  Sullivan Co., 72
MITCHELL, 39
MOBLEY, 96
Modoc Co., CA, 69
MOLYNEAUX, 28
Mongolia Ont., 39
Monmouth, OR, 53
Monroe, 12
Monroe, OR, 23, 81
MOODY, 9
MOORE, 71, 91
Morgan Co., IL, 10
Morgan Co., OH, 34
MORRIS, 37, 71
Mortensville, OH, 23
MOSES, 25-6
MOSS, 12, 46-7
MURPHY, 49
Muscatine Co., IA,
  79
MUSGRAVE, 31
MYERS, 1

NASH, 12, 85
NATION, 4
Nebraska
  Grand Island, 53
  Nebraska City, 51
Nebraska City, NB,
  51
New Virginia, 30
New York, 12, 19
  Chaney Valley, 12
New York City, 17,
  69

NEWE, 9
Newport, 81
NEWTON, 31, 75, 84, 86
NICHOLS, 9, 47
Noble Co., CA, 49
NOTS, 86

Oakesdale, WA, 23, 86
Ohio, 4, 19, 67, 79
  Butler Co., 12
  Callie Co. see Gallia Co.
  Champaign Co., 89
  Clark Co., 88
  Coshocton Co., 28, 60, 65
  Fayette, 23
  Fayette Co., 30
  Franklin Co., 89
  Galle Co. see Gallia Co.
  Gallia Co., 23, 66
  Licking Co., 86
  Morgan Co., 34
  Mortensville, 23
  Shelby Co., 30
OLMSTEAD, 66
OLSON, 86
Ontario
  Goodwood, 39
  Mongolia, 39
Oregon, 19
  Albany, 2
  Alsea, 91
  Amity, 84
  Ashland, 10
  Bellfountain, 19
  Benton Co., 12, 16-7, 23, 34, 71, 76, 81, 85, 86, 91, 94
  C. Lake, 88
  Calapooga, 10
  Coos Bay, 91

Oregon
  Coquille, 91
  Corvallis, 2, 26, 31, 71, 83-5, 89, 94
  Eola, 57
  Eugene, 37
  Eugene City, 12
  Independence, 56-7
  Jackson Co., 49
  Jacksonville, 49
  Josephine Co., 10
  Klamath Co., 83
  Lake Co., 67, 96
  Lakeview, 67, 69
  Lane Co., 12
  Linn Co., 2, 10, 45-6, 49
  Monmouth, 53
  Monroe, 23, 81
  Oregon City, 91
  Paisley, 96
  Philomath, 71, 81, 86
  Polk Co., 53, 57
  Portland, 58, 81
  Salem, 10, 57
  Sublimity, 89
  Summer Lake, 69
  Sweet Home, 45
  The Dalles, 10
  Wasco Co., 10
  Willamette Valley, 23
  Williams, 10
  Yamhill Co., 72
Oregon City, OR, 91
Oregon Territory, 10, 12, 76
  Benton Co., 30
Oreville, CA, 69
Orleans Co., VT, 65
OVERHOLSER, 4

Paisley, OR, 96
PALMER, 19

Paris, France, 28
Park Co., IN, 28
Paradise, CA, 69
PARKINSON, 79
PELL, 43
Pendleton Co., VA, 30, 89
Pennsylvania, 12, 19, 72, 79, 91
  Wilkes-Barr, 96
Peoria, 40
Perrydale, 12
Philomath, 75, 95
Philomath, OR, 71, 81, 86
Pike Co., MO, 84
Pine Grove, 40
Pine Knob, AR, 26
Platte Co., MO, 77
POLEY, 46
Polk Co., OR, 53, 57
POLLOCK, 66
POOR, 65
Pope Co., AR, 25
Port Townsend, WA, 10
PORTER, 37
Portland, 12
Portland, OR, 58, 81
Pottawattamie Co., IA, 1
POWELL, 4, 9
Prairie Grove, AR, 26
PRICE, 43
PROPST, 4

RAMSEY, 4, 53
REAMER, 28
Red Bluff, CA, 53
REEVES, 73
REYNOLDS, 79
RIBILEN, 43
RICE, 47, 94
RICHARDSON, 2
RICKARD, 16, 31

RICKERT, 2
RIGLET, 91
ROBERTSON, 39
ROBINETT, 49
ROBINSON, 53
Rome, WI, 50
Roseburg, 91
ROWLAND, 12
RUMMEL, 50
Rutland, FL, 53
RYAN, 47
RYBOLT, 1
RYCRAFT, 12, 19

Sac Co., IA, 28
SAFLEY, 2
Salem, OR, 10, 57
Salina Co., MO, 96
San Antonio, TX, 26
San Francisco, CA, 69
Santa Barbara, CA, 40
SCHMINCK, 60
SCHWAR, 4
Schwerin, GY, 69
SCOTT, 28, 77
SCRUGGS, 16
SEARBERY, 4
Seattle, WA, 40
SEITS, 12
SEITZ, 52
SELLERS, 60
Shelby Co., OH, 30
Sheriton, IA. see Chariton, IA
SHIME, 4
SIMLER, 19
SIMPSON, 12
SINGLETON, 58
Sioux City, IA, 28
SKIDMORE, 9
SLATER, 17, 19
SMALL, 4
SMALLWOOD, 4

SMITH, 17, 40, 58,
  60, 64-5, 68
SNELL, 39
Sonoma, CA, 69
South Dakota
  Glendale, 28
  Hand Co., 28
  Miller, 28
SOUTHERLAND, 4
SOUTHMAYED, 24, 26
SPOONER, 64
St. Clair Co., MO,
  47
St. Joe, MO, 23, 91
STANLEY, 53
STARR, 12, 19, 31,
  73
STEPHENSON, 10
STEWART, 50
Stockton, 69
Stone Coal Valley,
  CA, 69
Storm Lake, IA, 28
STRAHLEM, 52
Sublimity, 77, 89
Sullivan Co., MO, 72
Summer Lake, OR, 69
SUNDBORG, 57
Sussex Co., EN, 69
Sweet Home, OR, 45

Talene, 10
TAYLOR, 4, 9, 91
TERHUNE, 51

Texas
  San Antonio, 26
The Dalles, OR, 10
THOMPSON, 31
TIGARD, 12
Tippecanoe, 79
TUCKER, 67
TULLOCK, 67
TYCER, 35
TYLER, 68

UMPHREY, 2
Upper Canada, 17

Van Buren, AR, 25-6
Van Buren Co., IA,
  12
Vermillion Co., IN,
  28, 89
Vermont, 17, 60
  Brownington, 65
  Orleans Co., 65
VICTORIA (QUEEN), 24
VIDITO, 19
Virgina, 4
  Pendleton Co., 30,
  89

Waitsburg, WA, 94
Walla Walla, 77
WALLACE, 24, 26
WALLER, 57
WALTER, 12
WALTERS, 60
WARD, 24, 26
WARNER, 23
Warren Co., IA, 79
Wasco Co., OR, 10
Washington, 91
  Farmington, 23
  Oakesdale, 23, 86
  Port Townsend, 10
  Seattle, 40
  Waitsburg, 95
  Whitman Co., 23,
  86
WATSON, 25-6
WATT, 72
WAUGH, 66
WEAVRY. 35
WELLS, 56
WEST, 95
WHALEY, 86
WHITE, 64, 84
Whitman Co., WA, 23,
  86
WILEY, 43, 45

Wilkes-Barr, PA, 96
Willamette Valley,
  OR, 23
Williams, 19, 25
Williams, OR, 10
WILLIAMSON, 26
WILLSON, 91
WILSON, 9, 25-6, 53, 57
Wisconsin, 67
  Jeff. Co., 50
  Rome, 50

WOLSON, 86
WOOD, 19, 76, 86
Woodbine, IA, 10
WOODS, 64
WRIGHT, 4
WYARD, 23
WYATT, 12
WYRICK, 12

Yamhill Co., OR, 72
YORK, 72
YOUNG, 53, 91

www.ingramcontent.com/pod-product-compliance
Lightning Source LLC
Chambersburg PA
CBHW070932160426
43193CB00011B/1666